RELEASED

Journeys from prison to faith and hope

Alive Publishing

RELEASED

Journeys from prison to faith and hope

GREG WATTS

First published in 2005 by Alive Publishing Ltd.
Graphic House, 124 City Road, Stoke on Trent ST4 2PH
Tel: +44 (0) 1782 745600.   Fax: +44 (0) 1782 745500
www.biblealive.co.uk   e-mail:editor@biblealive.co.uk

Printed in Spain by Bookprint, S.L.

ISBN 0-9540335-6-6

I would like to thank each person in the book for agreeing to share their story with me. Each of them has done this, I know, so that others, especially those in prison, may find hope and be inspired to take the first step, or further steps, on the journey of faith. I would also like to thank Sister Carmel Fennessy, who was part of the chaplaincy team at HMP Wakefield for many years, Peter Henhegan, Roman Catholic Chaplain at HMP Wandsworth, David Payne, Director of Catholic Evangelisation Services, and Dave Vann of *Faithworks* for the help they have given to me. Finally, thanks to Mike Conway of *Alive Publishing* for having the vision to publish *Released.*

Contents

Foreword   i

Introduction   iii

Bernard   1

Alan Mortlock   9

James Rebecchie   21

Derrick Tranter   29

Andy Atkinson   37

John Pridmore   47

George Strange   59

Vijaykumar Raj   69

Tom   75

Bob Turney   85

Tony Sapiano   97

Foreword

Each of these stories is unique. Yet a common thread runs through them: of rehabilitation and faith; an open heart and the possibility of change. With this comes a sense of personal responsibility and a concern for others.

People are in prison for the crimes they have committed. They are given a series of challenges and opportunities, and when they are taken it is possible to begin to restore what has been damaged and to change life for the better.

People of faith, who work in our prisons, are signs of Hope. They encourage those in their care to face the consequences of their actions and learn to understand the reasons behind the crimes they have committed. This can lead to change - change that involves taking control of life and using that life to accomplish something positive. The people in these stories have turned their experience of crime and imprisonment into strengths, enabling them to put something back and make a positive contribution.

These stories can inspire others: offenders in search of a life away from crime; and citizens who long for a safe place to live. They prove that change is possible and give us a glimpse of just what can be achieved.

Paul Goggins MP
Prison Minister

Introduction

The first time I ever visited a prison was in my late teens when a friend of mine was convicted of assault and sent to HMP Leicester. It wasn't his first offence. Up until then, my only knowledge of life behind bars had been gleaned from the popular TV sitcom *Porridge*.

Situated on the edge of the city centre, the Victorian prison looked like a kind of medieval fortress. After being booked in at the reception, I was led by a prison officer to the visitors room, a scruffy and spartan place. My friend was sitting at a table in the corner, waiting for me. We chatted about various people we both knew and how our local football team was doing. I was shocked when he told me that he spent most of the day locked up in his cell. Leaving the oppressive atmosphere of the gloomy prison behind, I trudged back along Waterloo Way to the railway station, wondering how my friend coped each day, feeling despondent, and hoping that I never had to visit a prison again. Life behind bars, I concluded, was nothing like *Porridge.*

But I have been back to prisons many times, as a journalist. And most of my visits have been to write about the impact Christianity has on those in prison. I have interviewed prison chaplains, volunteers, educational and psychiatric workers, prison officers, governors and inmates. And on each visit I have been struck by the importance of Christianity, and religious faith in general, and what a valuable role the chaplaincy teams play. Behind the prison walls, faith often seems to be taken more seriously, and given more respect, than it is on the outside.

Whatever the tabloids like to make out, there's nothing cosy about serving a prison sentence, as Sir David Ramsbotham, the former Chief Inspector of Prisons, shows in his devastating and eye-opening book *Prisongate: the shocking state of Britains prisons and the need for visionary change.* Many of the 75,000 or so men and women locked up in prisons in the UK today live in an environment often characterized by overcrowding; a lack of educational and recreational opportunities and rehabilitation programmes; poor sanitary conditions; sub-standard food; violence;

bullying; sexual abuse; suicide attempts; drug abuse; and a labyrinthine Prison Service bureaucracy that often frustrates both staff and inmates. All of this, of course, is on top of having your freedom taken away and being separated from family and friends.

What a person needs, above all, in such circumstances is hope. In the film *The Shawshank Redemption*, Andy Dufresne, a banker, is wrongly convicted of shooting his cheating wife and her lover and sent to prison for life. He is sodomized by a gang but struggles to maintain his dignity and, also, his hope. He persuades the state authorities to supply him with money to buy books for the inadequate prison library. He also receives an old gramophone and a number of classical records. One day, while cleaning the prison office, he locks a prison guard in the toilet and plays a Mozart record over the prison's public address system. The men stop what they are doing and stand listening to the haunting music, which soars through the prison. Andy is overpowered by the guards and placed in solitary confinement for two weeks. When he comes out, he tells his friend Red that his time alone was easy, because he had Mr Mozart for company. Red thinks that he had the gramophone with him. Andy taps his heart and head and explains that the music was inside him where the authorities could not confiscate it. 'There are things in this world not carved out of grey stone,' says Andy. 'That there's a small place inside of us they can never lock away, and that place is called hope.'

INTRODUCTION

This book contains a collection of stories from men convicted of everything from armed robbery and assault to fraud and theft. They all admit to being guilty of the crimes they were convicted of, except for 'Tom', who maintains that he was innocent. The common thread that unites these men is that they found hope through Christianity. For some, like Bernard, this happened while in prison; for others, such as John Pridmore, it occurred after their release, and when they had returned to their life of crime. In many cases, what might be called a *Road to Damascus* experience occurred: when God broke into their lives in a dramatic and powerful way. Each of these men felt they had reached rock bottom in life.

In a society where culture and faith have drifted further and further apart, some people are cynical and dismissive about people who say they turned away from crime because they found God. But why should they be? To take this view is to deny that human beings can change, and in radical ways. The gospel of Jesus can be summed up in six words: 'Repent and believe the Good News.' And Jesus came not to call the righteous but sinners. The religious authorities of the time were scandalized when he ate and drank with tax collectors, prostitutes and outcasts, those on the margins of respectable society.

One thing a prison sentence gives you in abundance is time, something that, increasingly, many of us seem to have little

INTRODUCTION

of in the busy world beyond the prison walls. And with time on your hands you have the opportunity to think and reflect on your life. It is in these moments that the mystery of God and what Frederick Buechner calls 'the subterranean presence of grace in the world', can sometimes be glimpsed, along with our own frailty, sinfulness and powerlessness. As St Paul said in Romans, 'where sin increased, grace increased all the more' (5:20).

As the stories in the book show, prison need not be the end. It can be a new beginning. It is possible to rebuild your life and start again, especially if you honestly ask God to enter into your life. Of course, the crimes committed by the men in this book created victims. And anyone who has undergone a genuine conversion to Christianity is well aware of the hurt, or worse, they have caused to others. But no matter what crimes and sins you have committed, you are never beyond the mercy and forgiveness of God. As the American writer Philip Yancey puts it, 'God loves us not because of who we are and what we have done, but because of who God is.'

If the phone-ins on *Radio 5 Live* are anything to go by, however, there are many people who believe that the only way to deal with certain types of offenders is to lock them up and throw away the key, or have them strung up. But that is not the way of Jesus, who cried out in anguish from the cross, 'Forgive them, Father! They don't know what they are doing' (Lk 23:34). And a powerful contemporary example of Christian forgiveness was when, in 1983, Pope John Paul II visited his would-be assassin, Mehmet Ali Agca, in his cell at a prison in Rome.

The film *Dead Man Walking* tells the story of the relationship between the rapist and killer Matthew Poncelet and Sister Helen Prejean, who agrees to minister to him in prison. It isn't until towards the end of the film that he admits to her that he committed the crime and that he takes responsibility for the deaths of the young couple. She replies, 'You did a terrible thing, but you have a dignity now. Nobody can take that away from you. You are a son of God.' Matthew cries and says, 'Nobody ever called me that before.' Shortly before his execution, he says to her, 'I have to die to find love. Thank you for loving me!' Despite the terrible crimes he committed, Matthew had found faith and he had hope. Like the prodigal son in the parable told by Jesus, he had come back to his Father.

None of the men in this book would claim to be perfect – embracing Christianity is not some kind of spiritual plastic surgery. They still have their struggles in life, as we all do. In the words of Alan Mortlock, they are 'perfect men – under construction'. Even if you have encountered God on the *Road to Damascus*, you then have to meet him on the *Road to Emmaus,* like the two men in Luke's Gospel. In other words, becoming a Christian involves setting out on a journey of faith and having hope. And that is what each of these men who tell their stories has done.

Greg Watts

London, January 2005

Chapter 1
Bernard

When I phone Bernard and ask to meet him, he tells me that he always goes to morning Mass at his local Catholic church and then stays on afterwards to recite the Rosary. 'You can meet me there,' he says in his thick Northern Irish accent. 'It's not far from the station.'

A two-carriage train takes me from Belfast to the small coastal town where he lives and grew up, and I make my way from the station to the Catholic church. Although I've never met Bernard, I have no trouble in spotting him, kneeling in one of the pews at the front.

CHAPTER 1 - BERNARD

After the Rosary finishes, he greets me warmly with a smile and then takes me to his small flat, a short distance away. His living-room is full of holy pictures and statues: Padre Pio, St Martin de Porres, St Thérèse of Lisieux, St Joseph, the Virgin Mary.

Fifty year-old Bernard's life is now centred on prayer. He goes to the church twice each day and spends much of his time at home praying, especially the Rosary. While tattoos cover his arms, around his neck hangs a Miraculous Medal, a medal struck in 1832 after St Catherine Labouré claimed to see visions of the Virgin Mary at her convent in Paris. This is all a long way from the days when he was a member of a gang carrying out armed robberies.

One of five children, he was brought up in a traditional Catholic family. At the age of twelve he began breaking into houses and getting involved in petty crime. He left school with no idea about what he wanted to do with his life. He worked as a barman, textile worker and builder.

In 1972, at the age of nineteen, he packed his bags and went to live and work in Douglas, Isle of Man. 'I had been brought up a Catholic but when I went to the Isle of Man I stopped going to Mass and sort of drifted away from my faith,' he says. After stealing a bathroom suite from a builder who refused to pay him for the work he had done, he was sent to Douglas prison for six months. His girlfriend at the time was pregnant. He married her while he was in prison.

Upon his release, he started stealing again. He was arrested, convicted and sent back to prison. But clearly prison was no deterrent. After being released again, he returned to his criminal activities. He was caught and given a nineteen-month sentence for theft and assault. After another spell in Douglas, he was sent across the water to Liverpool.

He now had three children, but his marriage had become rocky. After completing his sentence, he decided not to return to his family. Instead, he moved to Scotland, where he worked on building sites. He met a woman and she became pregnant. She had an abortion and he left her.

He then returned to Liverpool, met Karen and moved in with her. When she too became pregnant and had an abortion, he left her. It wasn't long before he met another woman. Once again, she also became pregnant, but she didn't have an abortion. Yet once again, Bernard walked out.

Bernard's life had become chaotic, aimless and rootless. In such circumstances, another prison sentence would only be a matter of time, given his criminal past. This happened when he was arrested for shoplifting. He was sentenced to twelve months and sent to Liverpool.

CHAPTER 1 - BERNARD

He left prison and returned to live with Karen, but he continued drifting. 'I was ducking and diving, wheeling and dealing and drinking heavily. I was a sort of middle man dealing with stolen sports gear, cigarettes and things. And I also used to have the odd fight in a pub.'

When the police raided the flat one morning, he jumped out of the window and fled. Karen threw him out when he came back home, unable to tolerate his criminal lifestyle any longer. It was then that he met Lynn, the sister of a well-known Liverpool criminal family, and he soon became involved in more serious crime.

'I got involved with a group of people who committed eight armed robberies over a period of eighteen months. I was involved in two of them, on *Securicor* vans. We went out tooled up. I carried a baseball bat with me. I didn't earn hundreds of thousands, but it was a nice earner. I used to drive a brand new Mitsubishi and always dressed smartly.

'Crime often starts off with trivial things and then moves to more serious things. And each time you commit a crime and don't get caught you commit another. Most of the people I mixed with in Liverpool were involved in crime. They were part of the underworld. They would have shot you if they had to,' he says.

CHAPTER 1 - BERNARD

But his criminal lifestyle came to an end in 1983 when, along with twenty-three others in Liverpool, he was arrested, and placed on remand for a year. He was convicted of conspiracy to commit armed robbery and sentenced to fourteen-and-a-half years in prison. 'When the judge announced the sentence one of my accomplices started crying. But I didn't say anything,' he recalls.

After a spell in Liverpool, he was sent to Strangeways in Manchester. 'Some of the screws were anti-Irish and they began harassing me. So I smashed my cell up out of frustration and the mufti squad burst in and gave me a terrible beating. I was then walked naked to a nearby strip cell,' he says. He was eventually taken to the prison hospital, where he spent eight days. During his time there, he began praying the Rosary. He also started going to Mass, but, he admits, it was more because it was a way of meeting other prisoners than out of any deep religious faith.

Coming out of the chapel one time, I picked up a copy of the *Catholic Herald*. When I got back to the block, I read an article by David Alton in which he attacked abortion. It moved me tremendously. I read it again and began crying. I knew that I'd been responsible for two abortions. I was heart-broken and consumed with guilt for what I'd done.'

CHAPTER 1 - BERNARD

Then something extraordinary happened, he claims – while he was crying, he saw a vision in his cell of the Virgin Mary. 'She said to me, "Don't cry. Be happy." I was stunned. I couldn't believe it. She looked incredibly beautiful. Some people have told me that I had a dream. But I know it wasn't. I was awake. When I woke up the following morning, I felt I was six feet in the air.'

From that point on, he adds, his sentence didn't bother him. 'I met a Catholic priest, Father Peter Wilkinson, and went to confession. I started at the age of twelve and tried to remember anything that I did that was evil. I went through all my life, section by section.'

He was moved to Wakefield, and while there married Lynn. He continued going to Mass and he also began going regularly to confession. 'I remember one of the governors saying to me, "So are you now going to start behaving yourself?" I said I won't give any trouble.'

His aunt, a nun, sent him a copy of the *Divine Office*, the official liturgical prayer of the Catholic Church, and he began praying it each day. 'It took me about five months to learn how to pray it. The priest had to show me how to do it. I prayed it morning and night.

I started reading the New Testament every day and I also prayed the Rosary. I went to the gym every night at

CHAPTER 1 - BERNARD

Wakefield and then I'd go back to my cell to say the Rosary with a group of other prisoners. My faith really began to grow.'

He was transferred from Wakefield to Leyhill and then to Crumlin Road in Belfast, and finally sent back to Wakefield. He was released in 1994, and returned to Ireland. By now, his marriage to Lynn had broken up because, she said, he talked about Jesus too much. Feeling that he wanted to become a priest, he wrote to a number of religious orders, but they all advised him to wait a while.

That same year, Bernard went on a pilgrimage to Medjugorje, a village in Bosnia and Hercegovina, in former Yugoslavia, which was plucked from obscurity in 1981 when six young people reported seeing visions of the Blessed Virgin Mary. Since then, the village, like Lourdes in France, has become one of the major Marian shrines in the world, attracting tens of thousands of pilgrims each year. Whereas the emphasis in Lourdes is mainly on healing, Medjugorje has established itself as a place of repentance and conversion. But while there, Bernard suffered a brain haemorrhage. He was flown back to Ireland, where he was admitted to hospital.

He recovered from his ordeal, and today he lives an almost monastic life in his home town. He gets up each day at 5.30 a.m. and recites the Rosary and then attends morning Mass in his parish church. In the afternoon he returns there to recite the Divine Mercy prayer. Returning home, he continues to recite various prayers. As a member of the Legion of Mary, a Catholic movement dedicated to prayer and action, he regularly visits local families.

'I was brought up a good Catholic. My mother and father were good Catholics. But I remember a terrible thing that happened at Easter in 1983. I took John and Tony, my two sons, back home to Northern Ireland and we stayed with my parents. I laughed at them for going to Mass and told them I was happy with what I was doing. My mother never cried, but I bet she cried when I wasn't there. She told me when I was growing up that, when her mother was dying, she told her that she would have a son and he would do great things for the Church. My mother thought I might become a Catholic priest.'

Bernard says that he has met a number of people he used to be involved with in the old days, and he has urged them to turn to God and away from crime. 'Once the Mother of God appeared to me I was able to forgive everyone who had ever hurt me. And I pray each day for those who I had rows with, robbed, cheated, and fought with. God's forgiveness is there for anyone, no matter what you have done.'

Chapter 2
ALAN MORTLOCK

For Alan Mortlock, it was just another street brawl. But this time, when a fight broke out outside The *Room at the Top* nightclub in Ilford, East London, he ended up stabbing a man. As a result, he found himself standing in the dock at *Snaresbrook Crown Court,* listening to the judge telling him that he was being sent to prison.

A stocky, shaven-headed, forty-nine year-old, covered with tattoos, Alan is regarded as the UK's leading promoter of unlicensed boxing. Apart from organizing *razzmatazz* shows, he also trains boxers. He was twenty-two years old when he was sent to prison in 1978. He admits that it was surprising that he hadn't done time before then, given the amount of fights he got into in and around East London and Essex. A former skinhead in his teens, he took up various martial arts and became a very good kick boxer. When he went out to the pub he would often end up getting into what he calls a 'tear up'.

His memories of his time in prison are still vivid, he tells me when I meet him at the *Peacock Gym* in Canning Town, East London. 'Looking through the window of the prison van as it approached Wormwood Scrubs, I remember thinking how grim it looked in the gloomy afternoon. I then began to wonder how would I cope with life behind bars? What's more, I was going to miss the birth of my second child. I tried not to think about it and reminded myself that I was only in for eight months, not three years. But, sitting inside the prison van, eight months felt like eight years.

'What struck me first about the Scrubs was the smell. It was indescribably awful, a combination of food and disinfectant. A *Screw* unlocked a gate and ushered us through. Looking down the long wing, with cell doors on either side, I suddenly felt claustrophobic. The reality of prison really hit me. This was where I was going to live for the next eight months. I shuddered at the thought.

'I was awoken in the morning by loud shouting, banging and clanking. It was deafening. I went out onto the landing and stood there gobsmacked. What seemed like hundreds of men, carrying bowls, buckets and trays, were running up and down the landing and up and down all over the place. They reminded me of ants. I'd never seen anything like it.'

He found it very hard getting used to being locked up for twenty-three hours a day, he says. 'Nothing had really prepared me for the boredom. I'd met a lot of blokes who had done *bird* and they'd told me how the days used to stretch out ahead monotonously but I didn't really understand it. To occupy myself I read horror stories by Graham Masterson and James Herbert, wrote letters or drew pictures. Sometimes I'd do sit-ups and press-ups. One time, I even went to church, just to get out of the cell. I didn't go back though, as it was so boring. But the time dragged incredibly slowly. I realized why serving a prison sentence was often described as "doing time". If you saw the door open or the spy hole open you felt, somehow, a bit freer.'

Alan completed his sentence at Camp Hill on the Isle of Wight, and was released after eight months. But prison failed to change him. It wasn't long before he was getting into fights again in order to bolster his reputation. He made his living by 'ducking and diving', which included anything from buying and selling cars to dealing in small amounts of drugs. He then turned to organizing and promoting kick-boxing and Thai-boxing shows and found he could fill halls and sports centres to capacity. But soon his new-found skill and reputation took a back seat to alcohol, and he began to spend more and more time in the pub. Also, his marriage hit the rocks.

What changed Alan's life was when an ex-drug-smuggler friend came to see him at his home in the East End one afternoon. 'At that point, my life was in a mess. I was in the pub every day, doing drugs, getting into fights and Laura, my wife, had told me she was going to leave me and take the kids. Then a mate who had dealt in drugs big time came to see me and he told me that he'd become a Christian. He'd not long come out of Wormwood Scrubs, where he'd been on remand for the importation and supply of drugs,' he recalls.

Alan admits that he was very sceptical not only about his friend's sudden transformation but also about God and religion. 'I saw Christianity as something for wimps. But I figured that this Christianity lark might provide a way of my wife not divorcing me and give me some time. If I make out I'm a Christian, I thought, she might not ask me to go.'

Both Alan and his wife – who is Jewish – agreed to be prayed with and that night, in bed, Alan claims he experienced a supernatural event. 'I saw a man looking down on me through a haze. I thought I was going mad. I lay there feeling both excited and scared. I knew that something out of this world was occurring. The next thing, two hands were holding my head, and then I felt an incredible peace, happiness and joy, something I'd never experienced from drink, drugs or any emotion.'

This was the turning-point in his life. He began praying, reading the Bible, and, soon after, was baptized at a Pentecostal church in Leyton. He gave up the drink and the drugs and turned his back on his former violent lifestyle, something that wasn't easy, particularly during the time he ran a snooker club. He saw no reason to abandon his involvement with boxing and he went on to set up the IBA (Independent Boxing Association), which currently has around 300 members in the UK and Ireland.

Since becoming a Christian, he has been back into prison to give talks. He visited Ashfield Young Offenders' Institution near Bristol to put on a boxing demonstration with a young boxer – also a Christian – and talk about how faith had changed his life. 'I did two sessions, one for the 16-18 year-olds and then another for the 19-21 year-olds. When we began the boxing, all the lads began cheering and clapping. Then we went into a kick-boxing routine. Afterwards, I invited some of the lads to come on the pads with me.

'I told my story to the lads and then did what's known as an altar call. By this, I mean that I invited those lads who wanted to accept Jesus into their life to put their hands up. About twenty-five of them did this at the first session. At the end of the meeting I said to them, "Now, don't think I'm standing up here trying to be Mr Nice Guy. I'm telling you that Jesus Christ is real. I wouldn't travel three and a half hours to come here if he wasn't." I then told them that my son, Adam, was on remand in prison for assault, but that he knew Jesus.'

But the time he was asked to go into Pentonville prison in London to speak to Rule 43 prisoners – men in segregation for their own safety – caused him to rethink what he understood by the love of God, he admits.

'When I was told that some of them might be child abusers or rapists, my first reaction was to say that I didn't want to do it. But then my pastor asked me what I thought Jesus would do. Would he go and talk to these men? And I had to admit that he would. So I did.'

He emphasizes that while God hates the sin, he still loves the sinner. 'He is like the shepherd going in search of the one lost sheep (Lk15:4). Whatever a person has done, even if he's been the worst toerag in the world, if he repents and means it, and turns away from sin, God will forgive him. This is what Jesus did to the thief on the cross next to him. When he asked Jesus to remember him when he got to paradise, Jesus said, "Today you will be with me in paradise" (Lk 23:43).'

CHAPTER 2 - ALAN MORTLOCK

Alan prefers to talk about Christ-ianity rather than what he calls Church-ianity. 'A lot of the people who go to church are frightened to get involved with thieves, vagabonds or drug addicts. They don't know how to deal with them. I think that there are a lot of people that go to church and call themselves Christians but they don't know Jesus. They don't have a personal, born-again experience. In the Gospel of John Jesus said that we must be born again to enter the kingdom of God. I think that those churches that don't believe that Jesus can still heal today are stifling his power. He's still grafting as he was 2,000 years ago.'

He is aware that some of the people he mixes with have links to organized crime. 'I know that individuals from major firms and families come to my shows, and some of them are good friends. I don't think of them as villains or gangsters. I accept people no matter who they are or what they've done. I'm not there to judge anyone, and I don't get involved in criminal activity any longer. These guys know that I'm walking with the Lord.'

He often prays with his fighters, either in the gym, the dressing-room or in the ringside corner. 'I believe that God has called me to tell people about Jesus. I'm on the Lord's firm. When I gave my life to Jesus, I believe that God gave me the job of trying to reach people who wouldn't normally listen to someone talking about Christianity. My ministry is with the people who think they are the furthest away from

God. They will listen to me because they know I won't Bible-bash them and they know I understand where they're coming from. At the end of the day, we are all perfect men and women – under construction.'

He sees his job as sowing seeds of faith. 'I'm not a biblical scholar or theologian. I leave that to others, better qualified than me. I believe that God has called me to tell people about Jesus, but I'm not a discipler. This needs someone who has more time and patience than me. Put it another way. You could have a boxing trainer but he might not make a very good promoter. As St Paul says in his letter to the Ephesians, God has given us gifts. Some of us are called to be apostles, some prophets, some evangelists, some pastors and some teachers. My spiritual gift is to be an evangelist. I'm on the Lord's firm. Some Christians are there to plant the seeds and some are there to water the seeds. I'm there to plant them. And it may take a long time for the seeds to bear fruit.

When I gave my life to Jesus, I believe that God gave me the job of trying to reach people who wouldn't normally listen to someone talking about Christianity. My ministry is with the people who think they are furthest away from God. The guys I meet listen to me when I talk about the Lord Jesus because, before he came into my life, I was very much like them. And they know I wouldn't wind them up. These guys are my friends and, like me, perfect men under construction. I'll never Bible-bash them. If they want to listen to what I have to say, I'll tell them. If they don't, I won't. It's as simple as that.'

Following Jesus' command to turn the other cheek is not always easy, he confesses. 'I once lent some money to a guy who was in a spot of trouble. I didn't know him that well, but he assured me he'd pay it back in a few weeks. However, the weeks came and went, and there was no sign of the money. I spoke to him and he eventually gave me half the money. Soon after, he asked me for another loan. I agreed, believing that I'd get both loans back. But I only got half back. I felt annoyed at this, as he didn't keep his word. He was taking liberties with me, and I don't allow anyone to do that.

'So one evening I went to see him at his house. I said firmly, "I want my money. Just because I'm a born-again Christian doesn't mean I was born yesterday." I've never believed that Jesus wants us to be mugs. Part of me wanted to get heavy with him, but I knew this would be wrong, so I gave it to the Lord. I prayed, "Lord, I don't want to even think like this. I ask that you sort it out and that I get my money back." The next day, the guy did give me the money back. I have to be honest and say that I don't really know what I'd have done if he'd knocked me for the money.'

Alan is fiercely opposed to drugs. 'Some people argue that cannabis should be legalized. But if this happens, other drugs will be legalized. All types of drugs can lead to an early death. I know this because several friends of mine have died because of their heroin addiction or drug-related incidents. In the past, drugs gave me a buzz. But the buzz I get from when I'm working for the Lord is a hundred times better.'

And the devil is real, he insists. 'Don't let people tell you he's not. He's the great deceiver and the enemy of God. In the Bible it says that the road to destruction is wide and the road to eternal life narrow (Mt 7:13). When I look back to my childhood, I now think that my mum's alcoholism was something to do with the occult practices – the Ouija boards, seances, spiritualism – that she sometimes got involved in. And I think that the violence and alcoholism that marked much of my life was possibly due to a demonic influence. What's more, I know that the devil was trying to destroy my marriage through drink and he was making a good job of it until Jesus stepped in.'

To have a relationship with God you have to talk to him in prayer, he explains. 'This is the same with family or friends. Some people pray for, say, an hour a day at a particular time. I used to do this but now I don't. I pray as my heart leads me. I might be driving the car, training in the gym, or at one of my boxing shows. I pray any time, anywhere, any place.

'Reading the Bible is key in the Christian life, because the Bible is the Word of God. I find spiritual food in the Bible. If

I meet someone and they want to know more about Jesus, I'll encourage them to read the Gospels first and look at what Jesus said and did. The Bible is full of colourful characters. For example, Moses was a murderer and David was an adulterer. Yet Moses and David played a key role in God's plan to save the world. God can work through anyone, even murderers and adulterers.'

He says that he wouldn't have become a Christian if he hadn't undergone that extraordinary experience that night as he lay in bed. 'I'd never have become a Christian. And if someone like me had come into prison to talk about Jesus when I was inside, I would have laughed at them. I would have thought they were talking a load of rubbish. Back then, I thought all this Jesus stuff was for wimps.

'Because of the kind of life I'd led, I think I needed that knock-out punch from God. My heart had become hard. I know that some people will be sceptical about what I say I saw that night. But I know what happened.

'My message is that it doesn't matter what you are doing, have done, not done or going to do, but if you're looking for a change in your life, then you need Jesus. I know he's the only person who can sort you out. In the twelve years since I've been a Christian he's never let me down. He might make me wait for things but he's never let me down.

CHAPTER 2 - ALAN MORTLOCK

'You don't have to go into a church to find Jesus. You can pray to him anywhere. If you speak to him, he'll hear you and, if you ask him, he'll come into your life. He said in the Gospel, "Knock and the door shall be opened. Seek and you shall find" (Mt 7:7). We're all on a journey to God and are just passing through this life on earth. We all fail and sin, but God forgives us because he loves us.'

Chapter 3
JAMES REBECCHIE

E ver since I was able to think for myself I have lived an extremely impulsive and disruptive lifestyle. Somehow or another I was always running, always in pain, always searching. I have spent a lot of years trying to understand who I was so that I could stop hurting myself and those I love,' says James Rebecchie.

I meet James, a wiry twenty-four year-old, in Peterborough, Northamptonshire, during one of his periods of home leave from Sudbury prison in Derbyshire. On his wrist he is wearing two bands, a purple one with the words 'The key is Jesus' and a green one with the letters 'WWJD', which stands for 'What Would Jesus Do?'. His arms are scarred from the times he has cut himself.

CHAPTER 3 - JAMES REBECCHIE

He was born in Northallerton, North Yorkshire, the second of four children. His father was violent, an alcoholic, a rapist and a paedophile, he says. 'My birth father was not on the scene all that often. My mum divorced him when I was only three years old. He did not treat her or us that well. Our home was always the scene of some drunken rage or other. It was not the life my mum hoped for. My mind is filled with a lot of painful memories when I recall those days.

'It took me many years to be able to forgive Dad for what he did. I remember once coming downstairs in the early hours of the morning with my brother Martin to find Dad watching a porn movie on the telly. When he heard us, he picked up a knife from the table and threatened to stab us if we did not go away.'

When his parents split up, he and his two brothers were put into care. 'We had to stay in a hospital on the first night for loads of tests. The next day, social services took us to Richmond to the foster carers. We had to have more tests, at one of the local surgeries. No one explained why these were being done, but I now know that we were alleged to have been abused by Karen, one of my dad's friends.'

His mother got engaged to a former soldier, and James returned home and they moved to a village near Darlington in County Durham. At the age of seven they moved again, this time to a run-down council estate in Kirkby-in-Ashfield, a former Nottinghamshire mining town. By now, his mother had developed Crohn's Disease and she was in and out of hospital. James' behaviour began to deteriorate. He started smashing windows, playing on railway lines and spraying graffiti with an aerosol can. At school, he began getting into fights and sniffing glue. Eventually, he was suspended.

'There were many times when the headmaster of whatever school I was in at the time brought me home because of my behaviour. My dad would act like a loving parent in front of him, but as soon as we got inside the house I would get battered. There was even one time when the next-door neighbour knocked on the door late at night because I was crying after being hit. He ended up fighting with my dad.

'In my heart I was always angry, always hyperactive and upset. I don't think that at that stage of my life a day went by without some form of outburst or another. My home circumstances were what fuelled the rage inside of me. I hated my life. My angry outbursts were what helped me to deal with my pain. I had to survive the best way I knew how. The police and social services were well aware of my home circumstances, but nothing was really done about what was happening to me, my brothers and sister. There were many times when we all planned to run away, but we lacked the resources to pull it off.'

CHAPTER 3 - JAMES REBECCHIE

When he started at the local secondary school he began to get into trouble with the police. He used to shoplift in his lunch hour and after school and at weekends he and a group of friends would often go to some derelict houses, where they would drink, smoke and light small fires. One time, they set fire to one of the houses and James was arrested and cautioned for arson. Another time, he was forced to visit an attendance centre for a number of weekends.

'Gradually, as time wore on, I started to sniff aerosols on a daily basis. I was always feeling sorry for myself, always crying and always repentant when I got into trouble. There were many nights when I would cry myself to sleep. This was the first time I started calling out to God to help me. It was really frustrating because I knew who Jesus was. I had heard so much about him at church and at Sunday school, but I never felt that he was listening to me. I felt alone.'

Things became so bad that one day he took an overdose of paracetamol to try and end his life. 'At that time of my life I can't remember any positive role model. I grew up emotionally unstable, hitting out all the time, being rude, argumentative, hateful, malicious and really hyperactive. The kids at school nicknamed me "Satan". It wasn't a nice name to be known by, but it was a name. I was someone. It saddens me now that I once thought that the only way for me to learn was to be punished and taught some type of lesson. I don't think I allowed myself any love to come into my life.'

CHAPTER 3 - JAMES REBECCHIE

In 1996, he set fire to the bail hostel where he was staying and was arrested. 'I knew that there was no one in the hostel and I knew what I was doing when I committed the offence. I did it so that I would be sent to prison. I wanted to escape, because I knew I would kill myself or someone else.' He appeared at Mansfield Magistrates' Court and was placed on remand at Glen Parva Young Offenders' Institution in Leicester. He describes the ten months he spent there as like 'being buried alive'.

The following year, aged just sixteen, he appeared at Nottingham Crown Court and was found guilty of arson and being reckless as to whether life would be endangered and sentenced to life imprisonment with a recommendation that he serve a minimum of eight years. He had been expecting eighteen months. When he was led back down to the cell, he exploded and attacked another man waiting for sentencing. He was sent to Moorland in Doncaster, South Yorkshire. 'The biggest problem for me was that I wasn't streetwise enough. I was constantly bullied by people and threatened. And someone tried to rape me, but my screams were heard. Prisons really are evil places. I've witnessed a lot of evil things while I've been there. At Moorlands, I was always on a 20/52 for self-harm. I used to go down to the bubble to get a razor and the officers would give me twenty and tell me to cut myself to pieces.

CHAPTER 3 - JAMES REBECCHIE

'I gave up on God and became a Satanist when I got my life sentence. I cut stars onto my chest and played with a Ouija board. I would shout out from my cell, "Satan is king!" I began devil worshipping because I felt that God wasn't there. I had to believe in something.'

When he was invited to attend Mass one Sunday, he found himself agreeing to go. 'God spoke to me during that Mass. I could hear him clearly. I just felt so much at peace. I didn't feel that I was doing a life sentence at that moment. I felt I had something to hope for,' he says.

He began attending Mass regularly and, in 1998, was baptized a Catholic and confirmed by Bishop John Rawsthorne of Hallam. That same year, his case went to the Court of Appeal and his tariff was reduced to five years.

He volunteered to go to Arnold Lodge, an NHS secure unit in Leicester, on a two-year achievement programme. The course, which included psychotherapy, drug awareness, life skills, sport and counselling, changed his life, he says.

'It broke the negative cycle of my life and I was able to gain control over it. I felt that I didn't need to do all this self-harm. The hurting stopped because I was talking about it. It was out in the open. I didn't need to hide it any more.'

CHAPTER 3 - JAMES REBECCHIE

When he was transferred to Ashwell in Oakham, Leicestershire, he began attending a Pentecostal service. In 2003 he was transferred to North Sea Camp in Boston, Lincolnshire. Here, he met another Christian, Steve Jones, an ex-police officer who had been sentenced to life for the murder of his wife. They struck up a friendship immediately and Steve became a kind of mentor to James.

'At the time, I was into a lot of heavy metal music. I used to listen to bands such as *Slipknot, System of a Down, Opeth* and *Napalm Death*. When Steve said to me that the music was dangerous, I argued with him. But when I went back to my pad I started recording over every CD and tape I had and copying worship albums.'

Steve was a member of Peterborough Community Church in Peterborough, Northamptonshire. When he had home leave, James also began attending worship there, and he has been a member ever since.

'The church is like a family to me. After church we do a lot of things together, such as go to Pizza Hut or to the cinema. It's a great place to grow. You meet so many people and you can talk about your problems,' he says.

He finds the Bible a source of inspiration and teaching. 'It's an amazing book. When problems happen, you can find the answers there. God speaks to you through the Bible. I feel that I now know Jesus personally and my life revolves around what he wants me to do. I don't think you really understand what sin is until you know who God is. My faith has grown a lot because I have received so much support, especially at Peterborough Community Church.'

In 2003 at Grapevine, a Christian festival held at Lincoln Showground, he recommitted his life to Jesus and became a born-again Christian. When he was moved to Sudbury prison in Derbyshire, he joined a Bible study group. When he is unable to travel to Peterborough Community Church, he attends church in Derby.

Music, he explains, has given him a new lease of life. 'Music has allowed me to express myself. It is part of my process of healing. I can get a lot of the pain out through it. I went with one of the leaders from Derby Community Church to a church in Whaley Bridge, where he was due to preach. There was no keyboard player, so he asked me to play. I'd never done this with a band and in front of a crowd. I also gave my testimony. It was an awesome experience.'

James tells me that he will be appearing before the Parole Board in two months' time, but doesn't seem that hopeful that it will be successful. Nevertheless, he feels optimistic about his long-term future. For now, he says brightly, he has faith and he has hope.

Chapter 4
DERRICK TRANTER

D errick Tranter pauses and says reflectively, 'I don't think I ever thought of myself as a criminal', and then adds, 'And I didn't think of anyone apart from myself.'

I'm sitting with sixty-two year-old Derrick in the living-room of the small flat he lives in with his friend Philip in the West Midlands town of Walsall. This is where he grew up, but his life of crime led him to make fresh starts in, first, Nottingham, and then London, before returning to his roots years later, a renewed and reformed character after serving five prison sentences.

Adopted soon after birth, Derrick discovered at a young age that he was gay. He then found himself the subject of sexual advances from an older man. These advances resulted in him being raped on numerous occasions over several years.

'It had a dramatic effect on my life. This person was a friend of my mother. I didn't tell anyone, as I didn't think I would be believed. I was very frightened. Being an only child I had no one to turn to,' he tells me.

If this wasn't bad enough, he then slid into stealing to appease the man. 'He said that if I didn't give him money he would tell my mum. The only way I could get any money was to steal it from the garage where I worked. But this caused me a lot of anguish. Eventually I went to see Canon Dunn, my parish priest, and poured it all out to him. When I confessed to my employer that I had been stealing, they called the police and sacked me. When I told the police about the man, they accused me of making it all up and charged me with theft and gross indecency.'

He appeared at Stafford Assizes and was found guilty of theft and given probation. After leaving school at fifteen, he studied shorthand, typing and book-keeping at a local technical college and then got a job in the accounts office at a steel manufacturer's. He began forging cheques. Finding it was easy, he continued until one day he was caught by his employers, who were shocked to discover that he had stolen nearly £50,000 from them.

CHAPTER 4 - DERRICK TRANTER

'I spent the money on clothes and going to nightclubs. I had lots of friends and just went out to have a good time. I always paid. I began to have no regard for the law,' recalls Derrick. He was found guilty of embezzling and, once again, given probation. Because of the publicity in local newspapers about the case he moved to Nottingham, where he got a job in the office at a firm of fruit importers.

It wasn't long before he was returning to his old ways, but this time the judge was not so lenient and, at Lincoln Assizes, he was sentenced to five years' imprisonment. 'I felt embarrassment but no real sense of guilt. I suppose I didn't really expect to go to prison. I was in a bit of a daze,' says Derrick. After a brief spell in Lincoln, he was moved to Wakefield, where his homosexuality attracted the attention of a number of other inmates and also prison officers.

'One night I decided to end my life. I was getting a lot of pressure from other inmates and from prison officers for sex. Up until this point I'd led quite a sheltered life. I'd never mixed with any criminals. I felt I couldn't take any more. I stood on a table in my cell and was about to tie a sheet around my neck and attach it to a conduit when I heard the key in the door. I jumped down. A prison officer walked in and asked me what I was doing. He then talked to me and had me transferred to the hospital wing. After I came out I was given a job in the prison officers' tea room, which meant

I didn't have much contact with other inmates. I wore a red band, which meant that I was a trusted prisoner.'

Although he had been baptized a Catholic and gone to church as a youngster, he hadn't been particularly religious, but he began going to Mass. 'I returned to the Church because I felt I needed to get my life back on an even keel. But I didn't have any kind of conversion. Two nuns and a prison visitor used to come and see me, as I was very lonely in prison. People don't understand how lonely it can be. Because of the overcrowding and shortage of staff the education side, particularly in local prisons, is virtually non-existent. It can be pretty hellish being locked up in a cell and you will do anything to get out of it. I know I did. I went to Mass just to get out of the cell.'

After three years he was released from prison. In order to make a new start in life, he moved to London. A Catholic prisoners charity found him a bedsit in Willesden Green and he got a job in an accounts department and then with a piano manufacturing company, where he began forging cheques again. In 1971 at Southwark Crown Court he was convicted for theft to the value of £90,000 and sentenced to five years' imprisonment. Initially he was taken to Wormwood Scrubs and then transferred to Wandsworth and then to Stafford. After serving three years, he was released on parole in 1974 and, eventually, landed a job at the Institute of Bankers in London.

CHAPTER 4 - DERRICK TRANTER

In 1977 Derrick set up an office services business in Wembley. But soon he was back to his old ways, stealing over £20,000 from a sole trader for whom he was doing the accounts. He was sentenced to two years' imprisonment at Isleworth Crown Court and sent to Spring Hill, an open prison near Aylesbury in Buckinghamshire.

After his release, he returned to the office supplies business. But the lure of crime was, once again, too great. He didn't pay his PAYE and he opened bogus bank accounts. Two banks, Allied Irish and Barclays, took action against him and in 1987, at Snaresbrook Crown Court, he was convicted of obtaining money by deception and sentenced to five years.

He was sent to Wandsworth, where he met a student priest who was part of the Catholic chaplaincy team. He talked to him about his life and faith. He also started going to daily Mass and writing a daily journal. 'After work I would sit in my cell and read a small section of the Bible and then write in my journal what my thoughts about it were. I remember Bishop Howard Tripp coming to the prison once to celebrate Mass. In his homily he spoke about how we all have a service for God and that we all have talents, which we can use wisely or bury in the ground. This made me think.'

He continued going to Mass when he was transferred to Highpoint in Suffolk. One Saturday evening in November

1987, as he knelt in the prison chapel waiting for Mass to begin, something extraordinary happened, he says. 'I glanced up at the cross and I thought I was dreaming. What I saw was not the man-made figure of Christ but the human body of Christ. And he smiled at me. But he was in terrific pain. It's very difficult to describe in words. That smile totally and utterly penetrated the inner parts of my body and I instantly fell in love. I realized that, despite all my past, faults and imperfections, he loved me. I think really it was the first time in my life that I realized that I was loved and accepted for being me.

When I went back to my cell I wanted to shout from the landings that I was free. I had a conscious feeling that a weight had been lifted off my shoulders. I felt as if I was floating on air.

'From that point onwards I gradually started to remove all the walls I had built up. The major one was homosexuality. If someone loves you unconditionally, you want to respond to it unconditionally. But if you sense that there are things in your life that are a barrier you want to remove them. So, in the chapel at Highpoint, before the Blessed Sacrament, I returned my sexuality to God. From that moment onwards I have lived a chaste and celibate life. And the thing is, I've never missed it. And this was something that had controlled, or been a major part of, my life for so many years. Had

CHAPTER 4 - DERRICK TRANTER

somebody said to me that I had to give it up, I would have put two fingers up. 'When you fall in love with someone you want to get to know them. And the way you get to know Christ is through the Gospels. Jesus became a real person. Before, I was just playing at being a Catholic, because I had nothing better to do or whatever. At times, I had been a practising Catholic but I wasn't that committed.

'Had I been the only person ever to have lived after his death, then he would have still died for me. Other people will criticize and condemn me for what I have done, but here is Christ who is saying with a smile that he loves Derrick Tranter. Everything I've strove to do since then has been a personal response to this. I can now see that the importance of the incarnation was that God in Christ became Man. I can't have a relationship with someone in the clouds, but I can with a man.'

He and his friend Philip live celibate lives and are members of the Franciscan Third Order and the Society of St Vincent de Paul. They are planning to set up a religious community at a house he owns in the south of France. Derrick goes each day to a centre in Wolverhampton run by the Little Brothers of the Good Shepherd to help make food parcels for the homeless. His real crime was possessiveness, he says. 'If I hadn't have been so possessive I wouldn't have stolen from anybody else and I would have considered other people. Yes,

CHAPTER 4 - DERRICK TRANTER

I was sentenced by a court of law for an offence but that was the wrong charge. The real charge was being possessive.

'My past had been based on money, to buy possessions and friendship. One day, I was in the recess at Highpoint having a shave when I looked at myself and suddenly realized that the reason I was in prison was possessiveness. I never considered how many offences affected other people. I was totally and utterly selfish. I felt God asking me to follow him and be free of possessions.

'I know that I won't go back to my old ways provided I live day by day. Don't worry about tomorrow. Worry about now. But having said this, you have to be aware of Satan. As you form a relationship with Christ he becomes interested in you. Up until that point he's not been bothered because he had you anyway. I still have weaknesses. In Christ I've seen a real man and a man who is alive because of the resurrection. What happened to me had to be dramatic. I was only going one way, so Christ had to intervene in a dramatic way.'

Chapter 5
ANDY ATKINSON

'I thought this was it. I had blown it. My life was going nowhere now. With me in the van on the way to Armley was a guy who had been convicted of drug dealing. He said to me, "You'll be all right".'

Thirty-five year-old Andy Atkinson is recounting the events of 1991 that led to him being sentenced to four years in prison. He's driving me around East Leeds, where he is a volunteer youth worker. As he was born with no right arm from the elbow, no right leg from the knee and no left foot, the car has been specially adapted. Steering with one hand, he takes me around a council estate in Halton Moor, where he lives. At first sight the streets appear quite pleasant. There are no high rise blocks, just semi-detached houses with front gardens. But then I notice that many of the houses are boarded up. Andy tells me that it's a rough area, blighted by drugs and car crime, amongst other things, and that many people no longer want to live here.

Born in Leeds, Andy's father walked out when he was a toddler. From the age of two to ten he lived in a Barnardo's children's home in Wetherby because his mum didn't feel she could cope with his genetic defects. Throughout these years he visited home at the weekends. After Barnardo's he attended a number of special schools.

Because of his disability, he became the target of school bullies. 'There was a lot of hard cases at one particular school. Some of the kids thought I was an easy target. They used to call me names such as "Frankenstein", "Peg Leg" and "The One-Armed Bandit". This went on for about a year and a half. I told the teachers but they didn't do anything. They told me to walk away. But I found this hard to do. When I was punched in the face one day I hit the lad with my artificial arm and knocked him on the floor, and the bullies got a bit scared then,' he recalls.

When his step-dad asked him if he wanted to live back at home on the Cross Gates Estate he jumped at the chance. 'When I went home at weekends my dad would verbally abuse me. He called me "Spastic". The main thing that used to wind him up was that I used to have to eat with a fork, and when I tried to cut my food the plate would slide across the table. So I used to have to eat sitting on the floor. I found this quite traumatic. I preferred to stay at school at weekends, as the bullies weren't there then.'

He left school at sixteen and moved back home, hoping that life there would be better. 'It was hard for me to make friends. A lot of the kids didn't want to know me because of my disability. They thought I wasn't able to do anything, so I started shoplifting with them in the Arndale Centre to prove myself. I did this because I wanted to be accepted. I loved it when they did accept me and I could walk down the street and feel part of the group. Because I limp when I walk, I used to shove a lot of the things down my trousers. I would wear a thin pair of trousers, Sellotape them up at the bottom and put a pair of baggy jeans over them. None of the staff or store detectives suspected anything. They just assumed I was walking awkwardly because of my limp. I used to sell the stuff to people I knew.'

In 1986 he was convicted at Leeds Magistrates' Court of stealing a bicycle and fined £60. 'Then people started coming to me and saying that they had seen a stereo in a car in such and such a street and asking if I would nick it for them. So I began breaking into cars. I'd sell the stereos for a tenner. Then people began asking for wheels. In the 1980s wheel trims were very popular. I used to go to car lots to nick them. I'd sell them to a guy who sold them at car boot sales. My mates spent most of their money on drugs, but I spent most of mine on drink, mainly cider.'

In 1989 he was convicted of shoplifting from a car parts store. Undeterred, he then began stealing cars. 'One night in 1990 I went with a mate to nick a car and, after we'd broken in, he ran off. But I decided to take it on my own because if I didn't I thought that the gang wouldn't accept me. I reversed the car and my foot slipped on the accelerator and I hit a lamppost at fifty miles per hour. The car ended up on its side and eventually burst into flames.'

He was arrested at his house soon afterwards and taken to Gipton police station, where he was charged with dangerous driving and taking the car without the owner's consent. 'The police told me that they had witnesses to say that I was driving the car. Then they said that I had nearly run someone over. It turned out that a lad had jumped out of the way.'

At court, he was sentenced to four years in prison and taken to Armley prison. 'When I was asked if I wanted to be in the hospital wing, I said that I wanted to be in a normal wing. I was given a cell in D wing with an old guy. The cell was full of books and there was poetry on the wall. My first night was awful. I was petrified to go out of my cell for fear of the other prisoners. I had been bullied all my life and thought that the same thing might happen in prison. I asked myself how would I survive and I wondered if I'd be accepted.

'The next day, I was returning to my cell after slopping out when a guy called me over to him. He asked me who the old guy in my cell was. I said I didn't know. He then told me that he was a paedophile and that he and some other prisoners were going to do him over. He warned me to stay away. Two days later the guy was badly beaten up and taken to the hospital wing.'

But Andy received an unexpected visit from his solicitor. 'Three days later my solicitor came to visit me and he told me that I would be released in three days. I was amazed. When I asked him why, he said that he didn't know, but he thought it was because of my disability. The guy who'd spoken to me about the old guy asked me how come I was going home. When I told him I didn't know, he asked me if I was a grass. I told him I wasn't.

'On the morning of my release I said to the screw at the gates, "I won't be back". He replied, "Oh, yes, we hear that all the time".' Andy resolved to stay out of trouble and began looking for work. Despite attending a number of interviews, no one would take him on. He concluded that this was because of his disability.

'I tried to stay on the straight and narrow but I ended up shoplifting again with my friends. And I started breaking into sheds and nicking lawn mowers and shovels and things. I'd do it during the day and at night. In the day I'd usually knock on the door to see if there was anyone at home. If someone answered, I'd make out I had the wrong address. It's amazing what people put in their sheds. I once found a collection of old records and sold them on to a second-hand shop. But I never carried out burglaries like some of my friends did.'

In 1994 he got in trouble with the law again. 'Me and some mates were nicking some garden fencing from a garden when a cop car pulled up. My mates legged it but I was arrested. I was fined at Leeds City Magistrates'. When I came out of court I thought, "This has got to stop".'

Andy's life had, up until now, had little purpose. That changed when he agreed to run a football team for a group of local youngsters. He registered the team in a local league as Cross Gates Dynamos and persuaded Cross Gates Primary School to allow them to play on their pitch and train in the school hall. The Yorkshire Rider bus company provided a kit and someone else provided a minibus. Andy now felt that his life had some meaning.

Spurred on by his involvement with the football team, he undertook a six-month introductory course in youth work with Leeds City Council and then studied for an NVQ in youth work. 'After fifteen months my tutor told me that the work I'd done in my portfolio wasn't good enough. I'd worked very hard on the course. I loved it. So I walked out of youth work. This made me depressed and I just sat in my bedsit each day.' When Andy was twenty-two, Lee, a youth worker at a local church, invited him to help out at some events he was organizing. He did this for a while but then lost contact. Early in 1998 he met Lee again by chance while buying a CD at HMV, and he invited him to attend a church service in a pub. Andy agreed to go.

'The service was held in the function room of the pub. Lee told me that there would be some worship, then a guy would speak and after that we'd have a few beers. I stood at the back beside a pillar. The band played a song called "What can I do? What can I bring?" For some reason, I walked to the front of the room and began singing the song and raising my hands in the air. Then a guy started speaking about the lost sheep. He spoke about reaching the poor and people who have been involved in crime. As I listened to him, I thought that everything he was saying was about me.

'When he finished, I felt a peace I had never experienced before. I felt really happy and it seemed that all the bad things I'd done had been taken away. At the end of the service I told Lee that I felt totally different. He said, "I think it's God", and told me to speak to a guy called Toby. He asked if he could pray for me. I said yes and, as he did, I began to sweat. He then asked me to say a prayer, inviting Jesus into my life. I did this.

CHAPTER 5 - ANDY ATKINSON

'When I'd helped Lee with youth events I'd heard a lot about Christianity but I never really wanted Jesus in my life. I still had that criminal side to me. That night in the pub God met me where I was at. I didn't know what was going on, but I knew that I had changed.'

Today, Andy is an active member of Dayspring Church. He helps out at Kidz Club, a project for 5-11 year-olds at Bridge Street Pentecostal Church. Each Saturday, double-decker buses collect between 300 and 400 children from some of the most deprived estates in Leeds and take them to the church for various activities. 'None of the kids are from a Christian background. They come in and play games. The purpose of Kidz Club is to let the youngsters know that Jesus loves them and also give them life skills. They are very receptive, although you do get a few who mess about. But we don't bribe the kids,' he explains.

Apart from this, he is part of the Leeds Faith in Schools, which provides youth workers and volunteers for assemblies, RE lessons and after-school clubs, and he also helps to run Space, another children's project, in Osmondthorpe. In September 2003 he won the *Nationwide Volunteer of the Year Award* for the Yorkshire region.

'Many of the teenagers I work with are living the kind of life I used to live. But through my story, I have realized that I can bring them hope and show them that things can change.

Many of these kids are desperately looking for love and acceptance, in the same way that I was. It is important that they experience the love of the Father.'

Reflecting on his life, he says, 'That night I attended the church service in the pub, I realized that God had made me and that he loved me. I didn't have to impress him. In my teens, I tried smack once but didn't like it. When I look back now, I think that I could have easily gone down that road.'

Chapter 6
JOHN PRIDMORE

I felt like killing myself when I was in Hollesley Bay. I was really bombarded with my sinfulness and utter uselessness. There was no escape from it. I didn't have the sex, the drugs or the drink, which I had on the outside, so I seriously thought about killing myself, because I couldn't come to terms with who I was or what I was.'

Forty year-old John Pridmore is recalling his time in Hollesley Bay Young Offenders' Institution, near Ipswich in Suffolk. He was sent there in his teens after stealing from an employee in East London. He had already served three months in Kidlington Detention Centre in Oxfordshire for theft. Apart from a few days in Wormwood Scrubs some years later for non-payment of council tax, he avoided further prison sentences. This is surprising, given the violence and drug dealing he engaged in throughout his twenties.

'The days at Hollesley Bay were incredibly long and the regime worse than Kidlington. Unless you have been locked up in a cell for twenty-three hours a day, as I was, you can't really understand how long days can seem, just hours stretching out in front of you with nothing to look forward to. No TV, no treats, nothing. Looking through my cell window I could see the beach and the sea through the barbed wire fence. This only heightened my sense of losing my freedom,' he continues. 'Like many of the blokes there, I spent a lot of time sleeping. But when you weren't sleeping you were forced to think. The reason why prison can be very hard for some people is because they are haunted by their memories. And this was uncomfortable. I remember writing two letters, one to my mum and one to my dad. I told them I felt my life was a failure and how sorry I was for hurting them through the things I had done. I felt I had really hit rock bottom. What was waiting for me when I was released from prison? Nothing. I had no job, no money and nowhere to stay. And, of course, back then, I had no Jesus. My life was empty and the future dark.'

The son of a policeman, John grew up in East London. His slide into crime began when his parents divorced. But his spells in Kidlington and Hollesley Bay failed to change him.

CHAPTER 6 - JOHN PRIDMORE

A meeting with Bulldog, a former associate of the Krays, who had fallen out with them following the shooting of Jack 'The Hat' McVitie in a Stoke Newington pub, marked a turning point in John's life. Through Bulldog he began providing backstage security at pop concerts featuring artists such as Sting, Queen, Simply Red and Michael Jackson. He then graduated to working as a doorman at pubs and nightclubs.

He soon went from being a teenage delinquent to a vicious East London drug dealer and hard man, involved with criminals for whom stabbings and shootings were common. With a machete in one pocket and wads of money in the other, he enjoyed the classic gangster lifestyle: designer suits, sex with a string of women, a Mercedes with a personalized number plate, and a penthouse flat. He had it all – or so he thought.

Heavily involved in organized crime and finding himself descending into a spiral of violence, one night, at a pub in central London where he was working on the door, he launched into an argumentative drinker with his knuckle-duster and left the man lying in a pool of blood. He fled the scene with a gangland boss, convinced he had killed the man.

A few nights later, sitting alone in his flat in Leyton, he felt a voice tell him about all the bad things he had ever done.

He was, he admits, frightened. He recalls, 'I fell to my knees and pleaded for another chance. I then felt as if someone's hands were on my shoulders and I was being lifted up. This incredible warmth overpowered me and the fear vanished. At that moment, for the first time in my life, I knew that God really existed.'

What followed was a dramatic conversion. He turned his back on crime and violence, began praying, undertaking penances, reading the Bible and going to Mass. Although he had been baptized a Catholic as a child, he had never practised it. Following a spell as a volunteer in a drop-in centre, he landed a job as a youth worker on a tough council estate in Hackney. He then became a postulant with the Franciscan Friars of the Renewal in New York's South Bronx. After six months, he decided he was not called to religious life and returned to Britain, where he joined the Youth 2000 mission team in England and Wales. He is now a member of the Youth 2000 mission team in Ireland and lives in a Catholic lay community in Carrick-on-Shannon.

The work, says John, has been going well. 'For example, in Navan most of the sixty kids who came to the retreat were touched by God in some way. In Wexford, none of the kids had ever had a personal experience of Jesus. On the last day, ten of them testified that they had found Jesus in a personal way. At a retreat centre in County Galway, where over 300 people attended during the weekend, five girls told me they were going to set up a prayer group when they got back home to Tuam. Before I found God there is no way I could ever have spoken in public. But I've come to see that God never calls the qualified. He qualifies the chosen.'

So how does he approach young people? 'We go into schools and tell the kids how much Jesus loves them personally. I share my story and tell them how broken I was and that God loved me in that brokennness. No matter how weak we are God can use us to make himself known to others. As St Paul said, "For it is when I am weak that I am strong"(2 Cor 12:10).'

Youngsters are often unaware of how much they are loved by God, he goes on. 'Kids often have a low self-worth and don't know how precious they are. They are all too often told, particularly through the media, that they can only be satisfied through drugs, money or sex. One of the biggest problems they face is peer pressure. I tell the kids that all these temptations of modern life only offer illusions of happiness, because it is Jesus who is the way, the truth and the life.

'A story I sometimes use is that of the golden eagle. It's about a boy who finds an egg while he is walking on a farm. Thinking it's a chicken's egg, because it's the only egg he has ever seen, he puts it in with the chickens. But the egg is really a golden eagle's egg. The golden eagle's egg eventually hatches and, because he is surrounded by chickens, he thinks he's a chicken and he begins to peck around the farmyard all day long.

'One day, when he's out walking with the other chickens, he looks up into the sky and sees the most beautiful thing he's ever seen: a golden eagle. When he asks one of the chickens what it is, and is told it's a golden eagle, he says that he, too, would love to be a golden eagle. The chicken laughs at him and says, "You're a chicken, mate, so just get on with it".

'As the years go by, he carries on believing he's a chicken, because everyone tells him he is. But every now and again he thinks back to the most beautiful thing he's ever seen: the golden eagle. At last he dies and goes to heaven, and Jesus says, "My son, I so much wanted you to be the beautiful thing I created you to be".

'That story brings home to the kids that Jesus loves us, that we are created in the image of God and we are beautiful. When I was once giving a talk in a prison, a bloke asked me what was the longest sentence I'd had, and I replied, "Twenty-seven years without God – and it was a death sentence." The "chickens" might be our friends, family or the media. They can tell us we're no good and we need this product, this amount of money, to look like this supermodel, or to take this drug to be truly beautiful. It's deception. All we need is to know God's love.'

Since committing his life to Jesus, he has given a number of talks in prisons, including Maghaberry – formerly the Maze – in Lisburn, Northern Ireland. 'After I gave my story, a man came up to me and said, "I didn't like what you said about the paramilitaries". During my talk I had spoken out against paramilitaries on both sides and said that violence was not the way to peace. I looked at him and replied, "It's Jesus Christ who speaks through me. So if you've got a problem, take it up with him." He paused for a few moments and then said, "Respect". 'As I was leaving the prison, the priest who had invited me asked, "What did the man say to you after the talk?" When I told him, he shook his head and said, "Thank God for that. He's the head of the Continuity IRA. With one phone call he could have had you killed."'

He has also addressed the Prison Fellowship, in Manchester. 'It felt weird speaking to a lot of prison officers because when you are in prison they are the enemy. But afterwards I felt a unity with them and I realized that my hatred and anger towards them had been unfair. I hadn't seen them as people with families, mortgages, worries and anxieties.'

John's advice to those in prison is to use their time constructively. 'You hear about people in prison who have done degrees and bettered themselves. It's a great opportunity to read more and educate yourself more; to pray more, go to Mass and confession and read the Gospels. When I was in prison I read a great book called Robert Ellis. It was about a guy who committed a double murder and how he had found God. It really inspired me.

'If you want peace you have to go to confession. Speak to a chaplain. Confess everything to Jesus. Give him all your pain and he will give you peace. There's nothing worse than sitting in a cell thinking about all your sins day in, day out. It's easier to look for an escape route to kill the pain.

'Jesus sees our sins as needles sticking in our hearts and causing us pain, and he wants to take away that pain. And he does this in confession. I have seen the remarkable healing effects of confession in my own life and in the lives of many people I have met.

'We tend to limit God's mercy. If we've sinned four times in a day, for example, we think God can't forgive us. We place conditions on his love. We think to ourselves, well, you might have forgiven me the first time, and maybe the second, but you won't forgive me the third or fourth time. Yet God's love and mercy are limitless.

'When Peter asked Jesus how many times he should forgive someone who had wronged him, Jesus replied, "I don't say seven times, but seventy-seven times" (Mt 18:22). We must be like God and never stop forgiving. As I told Bulldog, God will never refuse even the worst sinner in the world if you say you're sorry. St Thérèse of Lisieux once said that, if she woke up one morning and found she'd committed all the sins it was possible to commit, they would all be as a single drop of water falling into the mouth of a live volcano, which would be God's mercy.' John describes himself as a very broken individual. 'Someone once prayed over me and they saw an image of a boat that had been shot to bits. Its sail was in rags. Behind it was a gigantic net and the boat was catching all these fish. When they told me this, I smiled and said, "That's definitely me". Most of the time I can't believe that God can use me like he does. I often feel a hypocrite when I'm talking about God. But I get back up when I fall. One of the saints said Jesus told him if he fell a million times he'd forgive him on the millionth time as much as the first time. If you wait until you're ready to serve God, you'll never be ready. Serve him now, even in your brokenness and weakness.

'Many people find they can't open their hearts to Jesus because of wounds from their life, wounds that affect how they live their lives now. We all have wounds, and we all inflict wounds on others. We all have to be healed of the wounds that others have inflicted on us, just as we have to be forgiven for the wounds we've inflicted on others.

'If you're someone with an addiction, say, perhaps to drugs, drink or even sex, then you have to be honest about who you are and ask Jesus to help you overcome this weakness. He will be powerless not to help you, if you really do want to change your life and you trust that he can do it.'

The change doesn't happen overnight, however, he emphasizes. 'When I first found God, I still carried on smoking dope, being aggressive and sleeping around. Slowly he changed my life, but I still struggle, even today. Other world faiths say that you have to obtain perfection to reach God. The Christian message is quite different. The Christian message says that God loves us so much that he came to be one of us and that he will bring us to him.'

Prayer is key in the spiritual life, he insists, but he admits that he doesn't always find it easy. 'It often feels like pulling teeth. I need to be encouraged by others to spend time in prayer. I've also discovered the importance of having discipline in prayer, of trying to pray each day at set times. When you don't want to pray, it's usually when you need to pray the most. A priest once said to me, "When prayer is hardest, it's then when we get most grace and blessings".

'If I hadn't of changed, there was only two ways I'd have ended up: doing life in prison or dead. My pride and arrogance were so strong. I wouldn't back down. A lot of people think reputation is more important than anything else in the world. It's rubbish. A mate once said to me, "No one's got a reputation when they are lying in the gutter with a bullet in them". And he was right.'

Chapter 7
GEORGE STRANGE

'I started reading the Bible and the words flew off the page. I had read bits before but it hadn't made sense. All of a sudden I was in a new world. It was amazing,' says George Strange.

I'm sitting with George in the River Christian Centre in Canning Town, East London, and he is describing how his life was turned upside down one night in Highpoint prison. He had been sentenced to three years for fraudulent trading and two years for manufacturing amphetamine sulphate (speed).

Throughout his life he had showed no interest in Christianity, he admits. 'One day the chapel orderly came to me and asked if I wanted his job. I thought that people who went to chapel were very often weak and you didn't know if they were sex offenders or not. They didn't seem to be like prison people. They didn't fit in. The orderly told me that you got £2.80 a week and only had to sit there, drinking tea and eating biscuits, as no one went to church. So I thought I'd take the job.

'I met Chas, a trainee Baptist minister, and he told me he was born again. But I didn't know what this meant. He talked about Jesus in a different way to other ministers I had heard, and said that he had died for me and had risen from the dead. As chapel orderly, I had to go to Bible study. One time, he asked me if I wanted to be born again. I said, "No, it's not for me". My mate Lionel, a former nightclub owner who had been done for GBH, also said no. He then turned to another guy and asked him. He said yes. Then Chas said, "Right, I'll pray for you but these other two can go to hell". In my cell, I started thinking about what he said. When you're not religious you tend to think everyone goes to heaven unless they are really bad. And I didn't think I was really bad. I hadn't killed anyone, but I had hit people, been a thief, a liar, a drug pusher. The next time I met the chaplain I told him that I didn't want to be the orderly any more.

'Then someone gave me a cassette of the testimony of Fred Smith, a rough and ready policeman. I lay on the bed in my cell listening to him talking about what God had done in his

life. While I listened, I started to laugh and cry. I didn't
know why I was doing this. Then all of a sudden I knew that
Jesus Christ was real. It was like a light going on. I knew
that Jesus was a living person, not a fairy story, and that he
had died on the cross for me. I started running up and down
the corridors shouting at the top of my voice, "Jesus is alive!
He's not dead. He loves us." My mate Lionel came out,
wondering what had happened. When I told him, he said, "I
want what you've got, George". Soon after, he became a
Christian and then so did an armed robber from Romford I
knew.'

The youngest of three children, George was born in a small
Cambridgeshire village, when his family was evacuated from
London in 1940. But when he was three months old his
mother decided that, despite the fact that it was regularly
being bombed, she preferred life in London's East End to the
countryside.

He grew up in Stratford, a tough working-class area close
to the bustling docks. As a child, he contracted tuberculosis
and spent the next year as a patient in Great Ormond Street
Hospital. At one point, the doctors told his mother that he
might die.

At the end of the war, his father got a job with Corrigan's,
travelling the country with their funfair. 'I can remember
going with my dad once to the Nottingham Goose Fair for a

fortnight. It was great because I got to have free rides all the time.'

George's first brush with the law occurred at the age of eleven: he appeared in court after breaking into a cafe. After leaving school, he worked as a lorry driver's mate and then collected and sold scrap metal from a horse and cart. He then went to work with his father on building sites.

The 1960s were, of course, the time of the notorious Kray brothers and George sometimes used to go to the *Double R* club in Bow Road and the *Regency* in Stoke Newington, both run by Ronnie and Reggie Kray. But he says that there was always a bad atmosphere and he never felt safe. 'You would be having a drink and then the twins would come in and you would feel the atmosphere change. They were violent men who, of course, shot George Cornell in the *Blind Beggar* on Whitechapel Road. I preferred after-hours drinking in the pubs.'

He also knew the Tibbs family who had a fearsome reputation in and around Canning Town. 'The Krays were more into organized crime and didn't want to involve themselves with gangs. But all the Tibbs gang had grown up together and were mates. The Krays paid their people and the Tibbs gang didn't.' At the age of twenty he joined the merchant navy and over the next seven and a half years he sailed to numerous countries, including Argentina, Brazil, the

United States, Barbados, Australia, Spain and Israel. Life was hard on board the ship and George, like many of the crew, hit the bars when they reached a port and often ended up in fights and other trouble.

'Once in New Zealand, I stole a Post Office van. I was chased through the streets by the police and caught. I appeared in court and was fined. The captain of my ship agreed to pay the fine and I had to work my way home. Another time, I was painting the side of a ship in Buenos Aries and another seaman who was drunk began rocking the punt I was standing on. To stop him doing it, my mate ran a paint roller down his arm. The guy then disappeared and, a short time later, returned with a shotgun and pointed it at me. I asked him to put it down. Fortunately some other seamen, seeing what was happening, crept up behind him and got the gun off him.'

When he came out of the merchant navy he got a job on the railway in Poplar docks. 'Our job was to knock things down. We sold all the bricks, metal, copper piping and everything and made good money. But all the stuff should really have gone to the railway company. All my money went on booze. I never went home until the pubs shut.

'I used to go out with Billy Haggis, who often carried a blade. Most nights we would get into fights and he would end up cutting someone. And Billy had shot people before.

One time, he had a row with some Custom House boys. He went into a pub in Freemasons Road, where they were drinking, and then ran straight out. They followed him and he turned around and began shooting at them with a .38. One bloke got shot in the leg and was crippled for life.'

He tells me that, after an incident with a man in a pub one night, he heard that the man was threatening to shoot him. 'I got a gun off a friend who was an armed robber. Billy Haggis came to see me and said, "Don't wait for him to come to do you. Let's go and do him". But this wasn't really my style, shooting someone in a pub. Billy said, "You go in the pub, call him out and I'll give it to him when he comes out". I went to the pub but he wasn't there. And I thank God for it because, if he had of been there, I would have had a long prison sentence.'

George then became a market trader and ran stalls in Rochester, Walthamstow and Roman Road. He also used to travel the country, holding sales in public halls, where he would sell radios, tape recorders, watches and alarm clocks. In 1980 he started working a scam called 'the long firm'. This involved buying a small wholesaler's and ordering small amounts of stock from other wholesalers. The early orders would be paid for to establish trust. Then a much larger order would be made but no payment would follow.

'Within three months I owed £175,000. I heard on the grapevine that the police were after me, so went to a solicitor and arranged to meet them. I was arrested and charged with fraudulent trading and given bail.'

While on remand, he bought another wholesaler's, at Shoreditch. But he didn't know that some men had set up a speed factory in the same building. One day, he discovered that they had been arrested. So he decided to set up his own speed factory, as he was running out of money.

'I got in touch with a chemist I knew and then went out and bought all the equipment, such as Bunsen burners and glass containers. He ran it under the pretence of being a company that manufactured picture frames. I knew that there was a lot of money to be made in speed.'

He had made one kilo of powder which he sold to buy better equipment. Pleased with how things were going, he had made another two kilos, but then the factory was raided by the police and he and his two accomplices were arrested – they didn't buy George's line that he was making perfume.

George was charged with manufacturing amphetamine sulphate and sent to Brixton on remand. 'When I got to Brixton I met quite a few guys from the East End. One of them got me a job on the hot plate, which meant that I wasn't locked in my cell twenty-three hours a day. Prison was just like being on board a ship again. When I sailed from London to Australia it would take a month and you would be in a tiny cabin. I didn't find it hard being in prison. Even though I had a young wife and a baby outside, I didn't really think much about this.'

He appeared at Snaresbrook Crown Court and was found guilty of fraudulent trading. George's two accomplices were found not guilty; he was sentenced to two years and sent to Wandsworth. 'I took all the blame because, if the three of us had been convicted as a trio, that would have made it conspiracy and the sentence would have been doubled.'

At Wandsworth he started attending Anglican services in the chapel, but not out of any religious conviction, he says. It was simply a way of meeting his mates. He reappeared at Snaresbrook Crown Court to face charges of manufacturing amphetamine sulphate, and was found guilty and given three and a half years.

He was transferred from Wandsworth to Highpoint in Suffolk. 'Highpoint was a relaxed regime, unlike Wandsworth. You could go to the gym and you could watch TV. They called it a holiday camp. I did art and drawing. I never realized I could draw until I was in prison. I carried on going to church, but just to meet my mates. That was until that night in my cell when Jesus Christ entered my life.

CHAPTER 7 - GEORGE STRANGE

'A few weeks after that night, some people from the Billy Graham Association came into the prison. They brought videos and literature with them, and they asked me to give my testimony in the chapel. I agreed and I cried again as I stood there, looking at the faces of the other prisoners sitting in front of me. I felt overflowing with the love of Jesus. I couldn't stop myself. The chapel began to fill up each Sunday and people started to get saved.

George's whole way of life and his attitudes went through a radical change. 'I'd always had a foul mouth, but when I heard other prisoners cursing and swearing I didn't like it one bit. God cleaned me from the inside, my heart, my mind, my thoughts. I didn't want to be angry, I didn't want to row, I didn't want to swear. I wanted to be nice to people and tell them about Jesus and how much he loves them. The Bible says that we are a new creation when we accept Jesus into our life.'

After his release in February 1987 he joined Elim Way fellowship in Canning Town and was baptized at a service in West Ham Baths. He became a lorry driver and then a chauffeur for a limousine company.

His faith was put to the test, he explains, when he was interviewed by the manager of the limousine company. 'When I went for the interview with the limousine company I had to produce my driving licence. It showed that I had been disqualified for drunken driving. The manager asked me how far I was over the limit. I told him I was double the amount. He replied that the insurance company wouldn't take me on, unless I told them I was just over the limit. But I told him that I couldn't lie. Now I was a Christian I had to tell the truth. I didn't expect to get the job, but I did.'

A number of celebrities travelled in the back of his car, he tells me. 'I picked up Moira Stewart, the BBC news reader, several times. I told her about Jesus and how he had died to save her from her sins. She listened and said that she didn't think that she was a bad person. I asked if she had ever broken any of the ten commandments. She thought for a moment and then said, "George, how presumptuous of me to think that I am good enough for heaven".'

Today, George lives with his wife and daughter in Dagenham and works as site manager at the River Christian Centre in Canning Town. He is also part of their outreach team that regularly visits Blunderston prison in Norfolk. He says that he is a completely different person to the one that made his living from crime. 'I look back now at my life and I have to ask myself how I did what I did.'

Chapter 8
VIJAYKUMAR RAJ

For Vijaykumar Rajah – known as VJ – life couldn't get much worse. His marriage had collapsed, and, as a result, he had ended up an alcoholic, sleeping in shop doorways in Cardiff city centre. Then, after being convicted of wounding, he was sent to prison. Depression engulfed him and he started to think of suicide. But when he found a Bible in his cell one day a new life began to open up for him.

He's now living in a small Essex town, working in a well known store and studying counselling and sign language at a local college. He has a girlfriend and a good relationship with his two children from his ex-wife. However, life is still not easy – he was given a seventh prison sentence, for contempt of court, in 2002 – but he now feels that God is directing his life. 'That last time in prison, in Chelmsford, was different. I knew Christ was with me. He took me through it again and I rose above my initial pain in coming back to prison,' says Vijaykumar.

While in Chelmsford he attended an RCIA (Rite of Christian Initiation for Adults) course, was trained by the Samaritans as a 'listener' and also got involved with the suicide prevention team.

Born in Kuala Lumpur, Malaysia, Vijaykumar had a difficult childhood. He was taken into an orphanage at the age of two and a half. When he was fifteen, his mother turned up out of the blue one day and took him and his two sisters to live in a council house in Caerphilly, South Wales. Forced to leave home by his stepfather, he joined the Royal Artillery when he was sixteen. While in the army, he began smoking cannabis. When he came out after four years he met a woman, who had three children. Eventually they got married and had two children of their own.

One of his friends was dealing drugs and soon Vijaykumar found himself being drawn into this world of what he soon learnt was big business. 'One day I went to the house of someone and I saw seven telephones in a small room and a man sitting there answering them,' he recalls.

CHAPTER 8 - VIJAYKUMAR RAJ

He became what's known as a 'tester', the person who tests the quality of the drugs. 'I'd go to Dover and Folkestone, where the drugs would be hidden in lorries. I'd put some speed on my finger and lick it. If I started behaving strangely, they would know that the drugs were good quality.'

In 1987 he was charged with affray and sentenced to prison for eight months after he and three friends got into a fight at a social club and a man was stabbed. The South Wales *Echo* referred to them as 'The Caerphilly Four'. After a spell in Cardiff prison, he was moved to Channings Wood, near Exeter. 'I made a lot of connections in prison and met people from all over the country. I didn't feel frightened. I found it interesting because of the people I met there, and I did a plastering course. 'In prison you either have to get on with it or wallow in self-pity. You feel very alone, no matter how many people you have around you. I missed my family a lot. Prison is a routine you must fall into. That's the only way you can survive. I always say, if you're in prison get involved in education classes or anything that will give you a wage. If you're a straight guy and you go to prison, you'll definitely come out a crook.'

He also dealt drugs while in prison. 'A piece of dope in prison is worth more than any gold. People will sell their wedding rings for it. There's a lot of violence in prison. If you're in prison, you should never get in debt, because you can get beaten up for a Mars Bar.'

Following his release, he became a drug dealer and also began using speed. He says he made a lot of money selling drugs. To conceal the fact that the money he earned was from drugs, he got a job in a restaurant. 'I supplied small amounts of drugs around Caerphilly and larger amounts in places such as Bristol, Bath and London.'

He then began handling stolen credit cards and cheque books and in 1989 received the first of three sentences for deception. When his marriage broke down in 1995 he decided to start a new life – living on the streets of Cardiff. He talks about this period of his life with great affection.

'It was a good experience. I used to sleep in a doorway next to *Debenhams*. I called it my bedroom. Cleaners used to wake me up in the morning and bring me tea, and a milkman would leave me a pint of milk and some orange juice. And some people who would go to the casino would often ask me to look after their cars. I became a sort of security guard. One day, two blokes woke me up at 6.15 a.m. and gave me £250. I thought they had won the lottery or something.'

However, he had begun to live life through an alcoholic haze. Each morning, he would go to the off-licence for his 'breakfast': half a bottle of vodka, three litres of cider and twenty Benson and Hedges.

Living on the streets has a more dangerous side, as Vijaykumar discovered. 'I used to play the harmonica to keep myself going. One evening, I was sitting in a doorway along St Mary's Street and I had about £4.50 in my hat. Two guys came along and one of them slashed me across the face with a knife.' He still has the scar today.

In 1997 he was convicted of wounding and given a three-year sentence. He claims that he was innocent, but appears to carry no bitterness about the verdict. He ended up in Cardiff prison, where his thoughts turned to suicide. 'I felt suicidal in prison because when I was on the streets drink was my friend, or my god. And I was deprived of it in prison.'

He went on a hunger strike, which lasted for four and a half months. 'Because I wasn't allowed a razor I decided to starve myself to death, and I went down from fifteen to nine stone. The prison, however, couldn't force-feed me like political prisoners because I wasn't protesting about anything. I just had given up the will to live.'

One day, he found a Gideon Bible in his cell. 'It was the only book there. I picked it up and started to read from the New Testament. All I knew about Jesus was about baby Jesus on Christmas Day who came to save the world and died on the cross. I decided to read a bit more. I became very troubled as I read the gospel. It started convicting me of all my wrongdoings. I felt it was just me and Jesus. I told him I was really sorry for all that I had done. But I thought it would be easier to die than to change. There was no medication or drug counselling that could help me, only Jesus.

'I read John 5:5, where the paralysed man, who had been ill for thirty-eight years, was asked by Jesus if he wanted to get well. When he said yes Jesus told him, "Get up, pick up your mat and walk". I knew our heavenly Father was saying that to me: "Child, trust me and I will save you. I will make you walk again."

'It was Jesus who helped break my addiction and set me free from all the guilt and pain in my life as well as the physical and psychological withdrawal. I haven't taken any drugs now since that time in 1997.'

So what would he say to someone who feels that they want to change their lifestyle? 'To really know Christ you must depend on him. People often say that seeing is believing. But it is in believing that I see more now. I believe I have a purpose. I know God didn't change my life for nothing. If people ask me how I changed, I can only tell the truth and say that it was the Word of God that changed me. Failure becomes a friend when it turns us to God.'

Chapter 9
TOM

T om (not his real name) had it all: a very successful business, a wife, lots of money and a big house. But then an extraordinary chain of events worthy of a John Grisham thriller led to him being convicted of attempted murder and conspiracy to murder and sentenced to life in prison.

Today, Tom, aged seventy-three, lives on the south coast, far away from his roots in the north of England. Despite a stroke in 2003, he is still very agile and very active. But none of his neighbours know about the ten years he spent in prison.

'I still have to carry with me the fact that I have been in prison and I still have to carry with me the fact that I was convicted. I was only released by the Home Secretary because Tony Benn wrote to him. If you look at the case that went to court in simplistic terms, it seems obvious that I was guilty. But when you put a defence forward it's pretty obvious that I wasn't. If the full evidence is not presented, then anyone can be convicted. In my case the full evidence was not presented,' he tells me when we meet at his pleasant house overlooking the sea.

Born in an industrial city in the North, Tom came from a working-class family and had a happy childhood, despite the hardships of the 1930s and 1940s. When he was called up for National Service, he ended up in the RAF, where he trained as an engineer and worked on jet engines. After leaving the RAF, he joined an engineering company as a draughtsman and then became an instructor in their training school while also lecturing at a polytechnic.

He then got married and began working as a music promoter. 'I'd always been keen on music ever since I was a child. My mum was a terrific pianist. She could play really complex music. Jazz was my big love. I had music lessons and played boogie extremely well by the time I was ten. The American bands who came over during the war influenced me a lot.' In 1960 he opened a club in a city-centre beer cellar. It soon established itself as a major venue, attracting performers such as Johnny Dankworth, Tubby Hayes, Dave

Berry and Jimmy Crawford, along with many American blues singers.

Buoyed up by the success of the club, he moved it to a former mill. With the likes of The Who, The Yardbirds, The Kinks, Georgie Fame and Joe Cocker appearing on stage, the club became one of the most popular music venues for miles, boasting a membership of 27,000.

But the demands of the music business took its toll on Tom's personal life and his marriage ended in divorce. He then met Ellen; their relationship developed and they moved in together. After five years in the music business he decided to move into property development. He was a success at this, too. He then began dealing in antiques and found that exporting items to the USA was very lucrative. By now, he had moved into a large house in a pretty market town in the Peak District, where he soon became a well-known and popular figure. Life seemed perfect.

But in 1987 his world came tumbling down when he discovered by chance that his partner was having an affair with a younger man. As bad as this was, there was no way Tom would have guessed the incredible events that this situation would trigger.

CHAPTER 9 - TOM

'He was twenty-one. She was fifty-five. She was flattered by him. But he was just after her money. She believed that they were going to live together, so she left me. I was shattered. I couldn't understand it. We had always got on. We had been together twenty-three years and we had worked very well together. We never had any arguments and we were both very faithful to each other. I loved her,' he says.

Ellen refused to come back to him. Soon after she moved out, he discovered that he had lost half a million pounds' worth of jewellery. What's more, she had taken with her the list of his business contacts in the US.

Then one day Paula walked into his life with devastating consequences. 'I then met a stunning younger woman who swept me off my feet. She knew of me and I vaguely knew her husband but not very well. I liked her because she was a pretty woman and she talked to me. I had been very lonely since my partner had left. I wasn't besotted with her though. I said to someone at the time, "At this time of my life I can afford a Porsche and I've got one".'

She moved in with him and within two weeks they got married at the local registry office. 'People who knew me couldn't believe that I had got married to her. We were so different. But I was so battered about what had happened with my ex-partner.'

A week after the marriage she told him that she wanted a divorce and half of everything he owned. He wondered if it was him or his money and property that she had been really interested in. He was stunned when, one day, she told him she was thinking of hiring someone to murder her former lover, a major drug dealer in a nearby city. Then he heard her say to someone on the phone that he himself 'wouldn't be around that long'. Tom took to hiding tape recorders in the house in the hope of incriminating her. But she found them.

Yet despite this, Tom still felt affection for Paula. He decided he would sell his house. As his ex-partner legally owned half of it, he had to obtain her permission. But when he asked her, she refused his request.

Tom told a fellow antique dealer about how frustrated he was with the situation and he suggested that he get someone to talk to Ellen. 'He said he knew an ex-army captain who would be a perfect mediator. My solicitor had written letters to her but she hadn't replied. So this suggestion of a mediator sounded like a good idea.

'So I met this guy. He was a very well-dressed, well-spoken man. I explained the situation to him and told him I wanted someone to negotiate with my ex-partner. He said he'd think about it and get back to me. He phoned me four days later and he said he had someone who would negotiate. He then told me he wanted several thousand pounds. I assumed that the man he was talking about was a hit man. When I told him that I only wanted someone to negotiate, he told me that the man knew the addresses of myself and my family. If I didn't pay, he would bump them off.'

Paula then contacted the antique dealer and asked him to make two bombs, one for Tom and one for his ex-partner. This way, she would get the house and all the money. The first bomb was delivered to Ellen. It went off in the courtyard of her house, injuring her hand, and Tom was arrested.

In 1990 at Sheffield Crown Court he was convicted of attempted murder and conspiracy to murder and given life sentences on each count. In addition he was ordered to pay £75,000. He refused and was given an additional two years.

'When the judge announced the verdict I thought to myself, "Something is wrong here, but it will come right. The truth will come out." It took me ages to find out that the man defending me was sleeping in my bed with my wife, who was the chief prosecution witness.'

For someone like Tom, prison was a massive shock. 'I was like a little boy going to school for the first time when I went to prison. I saw a pair of socks on the floor of the landing. I picked them up only to discover that they contained excrement. All the other prisoners who saw me do this fell about laughing.'

He soon developed his own strategy for dealing with life in prison. 'When anybody asked for anything I told them to take it. I was threatened by several prisoners. One guy said he was going to blow the legs off my older son. He told me he knew where he lived. And he did.'

After a spell in Armley, he was moved to Wakefield, which he calls 'Monster Mansion'. And it was here that he met prison chaplain Sister Carmel Fennessy while he was in the hospital wing.

'She asked me if I would play the organ at the Sunday morning Mass in the chapel. I told her that I didn't have any music and that I hadn't played a musical instrument in years. She said to me, "I'll arrange for you to have a practice".

'She encouraged me to go to confession, even though I wasn't a Catholic. So I did and I felt privileged even though it was hard. I was so grateful that someone would listen to me as another human being. I felt dehumanized in prison. I felt that someone cared for me. From this point on my faith in God started to deepen.

CHAPTER 9 - TOM

'I had prayed a lot in prison before I had met Sister Carmel. I prayed to be protected and guided. God is there to help us all but we have to make an effort as well. We can't just freewheel and expect him to run our lives. We need to run our own.'

He regularly read the Bible while in prison. 'I have grave doubts about the Old Testament. I see that as the history of the Jews. It's the New Testament that speaks to me. The thing that comes across is the kindness of Christ; his amazing judgement during hard times.

He was then moved to Nottingham, where he spent six years. He was put in charge of the workshop, something that helped him maintain his stability and sanity. He made dolls houses out of cardboard, papier-mâché, toothpaste and anything he could get his hands on, and also a wood carving of the Virgin Mary and the Child Jesus for the prison chapel.

'I was very fortunate when I was in prison because I didn't smoke, drink or do drugs. The governor at Nottingham said to me one day, 'You come across as white as snow. And I'm going to prove that you are not. I replied, "Well, you're going to be on a hiding to nothing because what you see is what you get".'

One morning, he received a letter from the wife of his solicitor. He was stunned to discover that his solicitor had been having an affair with Paula. After the shock had subsided he began to see the first glimmer of hope for getting his conviction quashed. It wasn't long after that he received a letter from Paula saying that she was divorcing him. She later married the solicitor.

A journalist friend of his began campaigning on his behalf and wrote to Tony Benn MP, asking him to take up the case. Disturbed by what he read, Benn wrote to the then Home Secretary Jack Straw, asking him to look again at the conviction.

'A member of the Parole Board came to visit me. The first thing he asked me was how I felt about the solicitor who had been having an affair with my wife. I told him I didn't feel anything. He then asked me whether, if I was released, I would continue to fight my case. I said I wouldn't and that all I wanted was to feel some sand between my toes again.'

In February 1999, Tom's status was reduced to category C and he was transferred to Ashwell in Leicestershire. In June, his status was then reduced to category D and he was moved to Sudbury in Derbyshire. Still with over six years of his sentence left to serve, he was released in the same month and placed on probation for just under three years.

One of his abiding memories from his time in prison, he says, is seeing Sister Carmel give and seeing the priests give.

'I saw how they cared for people when they didn't have to. One Christmas after the service in the chapel, I asked Sister Carmel how she was going to get home, as it was quite late. She said she didn't know. So I found a *Screw* who agreed to give her a lift home.'

He says that he feels ashamed of having been in prison and that since he came out he's become quite introvert. 'It's an awful thing to bear. People shy away from you if they know that you've been in prison. Being sent to prison is the worst thing that can happen to anybody. I have a friend, a surgeon, who served a life sentence for killing his wife. I met him when I was inside. He is now the pillar of the community in the town where he lives. But no one knows he's been inside.'

Tom adds that he has no animosity towards his ex-wife or the solicitor. 'Try as I might I cannot raise any emotion against either my ex-wife or the solicitor for what they did. This has puzzled me. I experienced his forgiveness in confession and I've been also able to forgive. But being able to forgive is a gift from God. We have to forgive and we have to move on.'

Chapter 10
BOB TURNEY

'If someone said to me when I was in prison that in twenty years' time you will be a probation officer, a writer, you'll be giving talks in Europe and America, and be invited to Downing Street, I would have said, "Oh, leave it out!"' laughs Bob Turney, shaking his head.

I meet him at the Moat House Hotel in Watford, Hertfordshire. He has come to the town from his home in Reading to have laser treatment to remove the tattoos on his hands.

Sixty year-old Bob might well be called a poacher turned gamekeeper. He served fourteen prison sentences in eighteen

years. Today he is a freelance consultant and trainer
specializing in helping prisoners change and overcome
addictions to drugs and alcohol, and he is also the author of
four books, including his biography *I'm Still Standing.*

Born in Carshalton, South London, in 1944, he left school
barely able to write his name and got a job in a furniture
manufacturer's. He later discovered that he was dyslexic. At
sixteen he was found guilty of taking and driving away a
scooter and driving without insurance, and was placed on
probation for two years. Soon after, he was charged with
criminal damage and being drunk and disorderly and sent to
Ashford remand centre for young offenders.

Alcohol had started to dominate Bob's life. 'Every pay day
I would go out and get drunk. I would pay my mother for my
keep and then borrow the money back again for a drink.
When I got drunk all the anger came to the surface. I would
put my fist through telephone box windows and cut my
hands and I would smash milk or beer bottles across my own
forehead. I just wanted to abuse myself. The rage I felt was
being directed inwards.'

He also began taking amphetamines. 'I had no confidence
in myself and the amphetamines gave me the self-confidence
I needed. They also kept me awake. I could go to parties and
clubs and dance and talk all night. For about a year I would
take the drug on a Friday evening and be awake until the

following Sunday morning. I would spend a lot of time racing around South London looking for drugs.

'Once the drug was working I would meet up with friends. We would make our way to the *Cellar* club in Kingston, or go to the *Marquee* in the West End. Both were open all night. They were the equivalent of the rave scene of the 1990s. Nothing else mattered. Only the music and the drugs.'

In 1965 he was arrested for office breaking and remanded in custody at Wandsworth prison for two weeks. He was then sentenced to three months imprisonment and sent to Pentonville. Soon after his release, he landed a job as a kitchen porter at Butlin's holiday camp in Filey, North Yorkshire.

It wasn't long before he was back in prison, though. This time, he received a six-month sentence, again for office breaking, and found himself returning to Pentonville. 'This was my lifestyle for the next few years. Going to the holiday camps in the summer and in the winter going back to the mail bags at Wandsworth or Pentonville.'

He got married in 1971, but found it difficult to settle down. 'My wife was very much in a world of her own. She would try to keep a nice home, but most of the money I was getting was going on drink and drugs. I was driven by my addiction. I did not respect other people's property in any way – it was simply there to be had to feed my craving.

'In the morning, I would make my way to the pub to meet my mate Terry. On the way I would do some shoplifting, stealing the most expensive aftershave and men's clothes, and sell them in the pub so that I could get a round of drinks. Then at closing time we would steal a car and do some house-breaking – returning to the pub for the evening session.'

In 1975, following a bungled break-in at a tobacconist's shop and a subsequent police car chase, he was sentenced at Kingston Crown Court to two years' imprisonment. During this period, his wife decided to divorce him. He left prison and returned to his life of crime, drink and drugs.

Feeling that he had hit rock bottom – he was now living in a squat –, he began attending a self-help group for alcoholics. A member of the group suggested that he seek admission to Pinel House, a detoxification and rehabilitation centre at Warlingham Park Hospital, near Croydon. He took the advice and, in 1981, was admitted to the programme. It was to be the turning-point of his life.

'I woke up early one morning in June and just lay on the bed gazing through the window which overlooked a green field over which the sun was rising. As I was taking in the view I sensed, all of a sudden, that the room was being lit by a warm glow and I was caught up in a rapturous feeling I had never experienced before. It literally engulfed me. A feeling of warmth crept over me and my mind's eye was opened. I could see that I need not drink or use drugs again if I did not want to. I had a choice. I knew that, if I wanted to be free of my addiction, I could be. A new world of consciousness and understanding was opened up to me, and a great feeling of peace came over me. No matter how wrong things seemed to be at the moment, from now on everything would be all right. No drug could have brought on this feeling. I knew, without any doubt, that I was loved.

'Slowly the sensation subsided. I am unable to explain what happened in that room. By now I was not taking any medication. I know today that it was a spiritual awakening. In the Acts of the Apostles in the Bible, Paul gives his account of his conversion (Acts 26). He was on the road to Damascus when he was blinded by a great light. I am sure that many of us with addiction problems have, in our own way, found a road to Damascus. Some people choose to ignore the moment of truth and go on until the drugs kill them or they drink themselves to death. Others choose to act and turn their life around.'

Bob chose to turn his life around. After leaving Pinel House, he moved into a hostel, passed his driving test and got a job as a van driver. He had also met Sue, who was to become his wife. She was a member of the Church of Jesus Christ of Latter Day Saints – the Mormons – and he began attending church with her.

He started praying regularly. 'I asked God to help me stay sober. After a time, I started to get some sort of stability in my life. I would hear people talk about prayer and meditation. I knew what prayer was, but as for meditation I thought it meant sitting in the lotus position, smoking a joint and listening to "Dark Side of the Moon" by Pink Floyd. I was told by someone that prayer was talking and meditation was listening. He said that, when I finished praying, I should take a few moments to be still, to ponder things and be grateful that I was free of my addictions.'

After a series of jobs, he became a volunteer with the Berkshire Probation Service. In 1997 he gained a degree in forensic social work from the University of Reading and soon after was appointed a probation officer. He now lives in Reading with Sue and his five children.

He spent five years as a probation officer in Berkshire before deciding that he could be more effective working independently. 'Let's face it, if the Home Secretary stood up in the House of Commons and said that as from midnight tonight he was abolishing the probation service, I couldn't see anyone marching down Whitehall saying, "Bring back probation officers". The old purpose of probation was about defending, advising and assisting. Today, it's about assessment and harm reduction. But the tools aren't in place to do the job.

'For example, in the United States probation officers have the powers of arrest and they carry guns. When I asked some probation officers what they did when someone violated a parole licence or probation order, they said that they would arrest them, and at gunpoint if they had to. "What do you do?" they asked me. "I write them a letter", I replied.

'I'm not suggesting probation officers in Britain carry guns but what I am suggesting to Government is that we have a couple of probation officers in a team who are sworn in as special constables. This would give them the powers of arrest. You would only have to do it a couple of times for the message to get out. When they sent that woman to prison for not sending her daughter to school the school attendance rates rose. And that would happen with the Probation Service. If people on orders knew we had teeth, the attendance rate would rise. At the moment, we don't have the teeth and the Probation Service is ineffective as a result.'

One of the projects he is involved in is for young offenders at Huntercombe in Oxfordshire. 'We go and start looking at the process of change. We take the youngsters through seven stages. For example, we give them a prison bag with clothes in it and ask them what they are going to do. They usually say, "Oh, I dunno. I might go on the road or talk to my boys." 'They're not children but they're also not men. We get them to look at things from a different perspective. I will ask one guy to stand in the middle of the room and ask the others how many eyes, arms and ears they can see. Some will see the eyes, others just one ear or just an arm. Then we will get them to move around so that they start thinking about looking at life from a different perspective. What we are trying to do is reframe their thinking about situations. You have to be very visual with the kids. You can't sit down and lecture them. 'We interview the kids before we start the sessions. We try and find out who they live with and who is at home. And it's generally – and I'm not stereotyping – that they live with mum. Dad's not on the scene or he's in prison. We start with about fifteen kids and retain about nine, which is pretty good.' Unsurprisingly, he has strong views on crime, punishment and justice, and is frequently invited to appear on TV and radio or give lectures around the world. 'When I was in prison I think the overall population was below 40,000. But we still had overcrowding and staff shortages. We tend to build more prisons hoping we will do something about crime. But that's like building more hospitals and hoping to cut down on road accidents. We're using prison too eagerly. When care in the community was introduced and they started emptying the mental institutions, where did a lot of these people end up? In the Prison Service. And the Prison Service is not equipped to deal with those kind of people.

'If you have been in and out of prison like I had, there's an issue of institutionalization. Prison can be easy for some people, because they have no responsibility. They are taken care of. I've talked to a number of mothers whose sons are in prison and they often say, "Well, at least we know that he's safe". 'Prisons are now being star rated, which means that we are going to get people being creative with their reporting. Huntingdon Young Offenders' Institution came out as one of the most violent prisons in the country. When I was interviewed by the media I said, "It's not. It does kick off in there because the youngsters are very volatile. The trouble is that the staff report everything. They will report play fighting as an incident."'

Alternative ways of dealing with offenders need to be found, he believes. 'For instance, with young offending teams they've introduced intense supervision and surveillance orders where they tag and monitor youngsters for around twenty-five hours a week.

He is also involved with the Prisoners' Education Trust, which runs correspondence courses for prisoners, and he was invited to Downing Street to discuss the charity's work with Cherie Blair. 'Prisons are very transient places. The courses follow the prisoners from prison to prison. Someone once remarked that a person shouldn't be sentenced to five years, they should be sentenced to five A levels. But I don't want a well-educated burglar or thug. I want a reformed well-educated burglar or thug. Education is important but you also have to have offending behaviour programmes. Some people go over the top with education and think that it's the whole answer.'

A major influence on his life, he says, was the late Lord Longford, a committed prison reformer. 'Frank had a gift of not caring what people thought about him. He just said what he felt. He came to my first book launch. He was always scruffy. I first met him when I was working in a bail hostel in Reading. I wrote to him and invited him to come and give a talk. When I went to pick him up from his home in Chelsea he said, "Tell me about you". So I told him about my life and then he said, "You need to write a book". I thought he was being ridiculous and didn't think any more about it.

'A couple of weeks later he phoned and said that he had been thinking about the book and that he wanted to write the introduction. He really inspired me and he had faith that I could do anything I wanted to do. If I'd not had his encouragement I wouldn't have written any books.'

Looking back to that moment at Pinel House, he says, 'I just knew that I could change if I wanted to. But this only came about when I realized that I wasn't the managing director of the universe, because everything revolved around me. Things then happened to me that I had no control over.

But when I was in control of my life I was taking drugs, getting nicked and sent to prison. Now that I was handing my will and life over to the care of God things started to happen.'

He confesses that he never liked the flavour of alcohol, but had always used it for the effect it has on his mind and body. 'It made me feel different. Many times since then I have heard people talk about "social drinking". Some people have said that they drank socially for five, ten and, in some cases, twenty years before alcohol became a problem. I drank socially for all of ten minutes. After that, there never was anything remotely social or sociable about the way I drank. For a long time the only thing I did was to drink badly.

'The first step is that we admit we are powerless over alcohol and that our lives have become unmanageable. They call the AA programme a spiritual kindergarten. It was a great help to me. It's all about acknowledging a higher power.

'I used to be an atheist in the old days. You used to get the Salvation Army officers coming round to the pubs with a collection, and I used to be very rude to them. I was very anti-religion. But if I go into a typical probation meeting and say that someone has no chance unless they have a complete faith in God, they look at me as if I'm completely mad.'

Help is available if you want to change your life and be freed of addictions, he insists. 'When I eventually said I needed help it seemed that people came out of the woodwork. They were already there but I was blind to them. Many people in prison have no self-esteem and confidence in themselves, even though they may have a lot of bravado. My self-esteem came through my conversion to Christianity. I will always be grateful to the probation service, as I will be for God's love in my life today, and without which I'm sure that I would be dead or in some long-term institution.'

Chapter 11
TONY SAPIANO

'It's abnormal to allow yourself to be continually incarcerated, because it's a terrible thing. I believe that, when I made that decision in the police station to stop thieving and doing everything else I was doing, God broke a spiritual stronghold in my life,' says Tony Sapiano.

It's a scorching hot June morning and I'm sitting with Tony and his wife Maria drinking coffee outside a cafe bar near Tower Bridge in London, close to where Tony grew up in Wapping. Today, Tony's a builder, having turned his back on crime some years ago following betrayal by his friends and a realization that he wasn't the man he felt he should be.

CHAPTER 11 - TONY SAPIANO

The son of a Maltese father, and one of eight children, he first got involved in crime as a teenager and served time in several borstals and detention centres. 'I suppose I was trying to find myself really. Back in those days there was two types of people in London. You were either a thief or a worker. It was all about trying to survive. Two of my older brothers made a living as thieves and one of them became well known for armed robbery. 'I was victimized by the police because of the reputation two of my brothers had. As soon as our name was mentioned in front of the police anywhere in London, it was assumed we were doing something wrong. The first time I went into a detention centre, at the age of fifteen, I was fitted up. I know it's a cliché, but I was.

'And it's like anything else. If you lie with dogs, you catch fleas. And although I came out still pretty innocent, I guess I'd built up certain attitudes, felt resentment and had a sense of kudos and bravado because I'd been in prison. And, of course, you keep in contact with the people you meet inside and one thing leads to another. I didn't plan to be bad. At that point in my life, I enjoyed the same things most lads of my age did. I enjoyed chatting up the girls and I wanted to work and earn some money. But I didn't really know how to find a way out of all this garbage I was in.'

He graduated to more serious crime, such as hijacking lorries, and robbing betting shops and houses. Sometimes he went armed and on occasions dressed as a police officer. 'I never set out to be an armed robber. People would come with an offer of work and I would take it if it made money. But I was a realist and I knew that there was certain areas that if you went into them it would be a point of no return. Although I never let anyone down when I went to work, I always had this sense that this wasn't really for me. I went wherever there was money. 'I always had a sense of God and a feeling that I would have to answer to him at some stage, but I wasn't too bothered about it. I was very calculated and cold. If I had to take a reprisal for something, then I would, no matter how extreme I would have to be. I would have been prepared to take a life if I hadn't of had this restraining factor. I think to take a life is the worst thing that anyone can do.'

In 1977 he was sentenced to prison for armed robbery. He was released after serving three years. 'I'd had one or two experiences in prison which I would call God orientated. I'd met a guy who talked to me a lot about God, but I took it with a pinch of salt. When I came out of prison I tried to go straight for a while. At the time, I was single and I moved in with a good friend of mine and we formed a business together. 'But one of my older brothers had been fingered by two friends who had become supergrasses. Because of the stress this put on me, along with other things, I soon found myself back in the mainstream of villainy. A friend of one of my brothers propositioned me on a hijacking. He had been charged with robbery and was trying to get £40,000 to pay his bail money so that he could flee the country.

'We did the hijacking and then some more robberies. But what I didn't know was that this guy was a supergrass and he was living in a police station. I never had a clue about this. He made statements about me to the police. I found this hard because I'd never known this personal betrayal. He used to come round to the house where I lived with Maria.

'I then became friends with Danny Woods, who is now doing life for murder. He was very heavy. I think he shot someone on every bit of work that he went on. He was a lovely guy but a bad bit of work. What I didn't know was that he had turned supergrass and had made statements against me. When I went to collect our two children from school the police were there waiting for me. I was astounded because I didn't think anyone knew my movements. I was already on bail. They pulled me in and held me for about a week. They told me my bail had gone whether I talked or not. I knew that I would be looking at about fifteen years for what I had done.

'After about a week, just before I was due to go to Brixton, I reflected on the situation and thought to myself, "I'm about to throw my life down the swanny again, but for people that are not worth too much." That week in the cell gave me a lot of time for reflection. I do believe at that time that God was speaking to me in some way. I had no faith in friends and no faith in the people I had put my life on the line for. The underworld code of honour meant nothing now. This was a big body blow to me because I'd cultivated this understanding that people didn't do this. I'd gone to prison for people when I had been innocent. I thought about all these things and said to myself that there was two ways forward. I could either go to prison because of what my wonderful friends had done or I could turn over a whole new leaf.

'I decided that if I was going to go to prison I was going to make sure that nothing came out of the woodwork when I came out. I'd heard about gate arrests; of guys doing five or ten years and then being recharged by the police. The police had never been friendly to me, so I figured they would like to do that.

'It was a case of self-preservation. I asked to see the chief inspector and I told him I wasn't interested in any deals or anything. I said what I want to do is admit to everything I've ever done and have it taken into consideration so that when I go to court nobody else can come out of the woodwork. The police agreed and they asked me if I'd be prepared to implicate other people.

'If you ever make a statement against anyone else, it's not worth the paper it's written on unless it's corroborated. I knew that I had to give an honest account. I never had any intention of going to court against anybody. I knew that evidence against other people I knew had already been given. I had to make a court appearance so that I could be remanded in custody for the statements to be made. The police didn't play straight, as usual, though. They put me up as a supergrass. But I wasn't too worried about it, as I knew that I wasn't a supergrass. As far as I can remember there was only two people who got in trouble, both good friends of mine. One of them phoned me a few days before I was arrested and offered to sell me a gun. I told him not to talk over the phone. It turned out that my phone was bugged.'

Tony appeared at the Old Bailey in 1979 and was convicted of armed robbery and theft and sentenced to five years, a lesser sentence than he had been expecting. 'While I was in prison in Norwich, I prayed and called out to God. I felt bereft of family and friends. A prison visitor who was a Christian came to see me one day, but he put me off Christianity and God. He was too emotional and I was apprehensive about this sort of approach. But I now know that he was just showing love.'

Tony came out of prison in 1983, determined to go straight. 'I'd been out of prison for quite a while and I was pondering the things of God. I didn't want to be religious. I gave myself enough time to know what I was doing. I had a lovely wife, lovely children, a good home, love, security, all the things a man wants, but there was something missing. It was obvious to me that what was missing was knowing who I was. I realize now that God was speaking to me and he had been for a number of years, but I didn't listen. I didn't want to be godly. I wanted to be a sinner.'

Seeking some signposts towards God, he contacted a man called Dave, a Christian who had prayed with him in the visiting room in Bedford, where he had completed his sentence. He invited Tony to a meeting of the Full Gospel Businessmen's Fellowship at a hall in Bletchley Park, Buckinghamshire. 'I believe that night I had an encounter with God. I saw Jesus as he really is and accepted him as my personal Saviour. At the end of the evening, an elderly guy came up to me and asked me if I would like some prayer. I replied that I would love some prayer. When he asked me what I would like him to pray for, I replied, "You name it. I've got a full house. I've got everything."'

In 1986 Tony was baptized at Elim Pentecostal Church, in New Bradwell, near Milton Keynes. 'My life took on a whole new meaning when I decided to become a Christian. God is loving, understanding and just. God levels things out. I believe he set the ground when I was arrested in 1979, knowing I would come to him eventually. I always felt there was a missing ingredient in me. An ambition to be somebody. But I wasn't bothered about that. I went on a moment-to-moment buzz, which often subsided very quickly. But I didn't want to be violent for the sake of being violent.'

Tony now lives in East London, where he runs a building firm. 'When I came out I met most of the people from the old days. Some asked me to go back to work with them and I had to tell them that I didn't do that any more. I've never worried about money. I've trusted in God to provide and he's done this every time. The real tragedy was that my family had to undergo the stigma that is associated with being called a grass. But only those close to me know the real truth about the situation. I wasn't bothered because I had made my peace with God and man and I had never stood up in court and pointed the finger against anyone.

'I've been a Christian for about twenty-four years and I'm far from perfect. I gave a testimony to some gypsies in Portugal and I told them that there had been two things that had run through my life: anger and rebellion. And I'm still dealing with it. I still haven't conquered it. I try to let God into my life. Sometimes he has an easy job and sometimes he has a hard job.'

DON'T FORGET PRISONERS
JESUS DIDN'T!

'It is great to know that there are people 'out there' who really care about those hidden away behind bars.'

Send a cheque (made payable to International Prison Outreach) to Alive Publishing, Graphic House, 124 City Road, Stoke on Trent ST4 2PH.

Or call our credit card hotline on **+44(0) 01782 745600** to make your donation.

International Prison Outreach is committed to supporting prisoners around the world. Please Help.

Make your donation today.